LOVE LESSONS

FROM THE OLD WEST

Other Books by Chris Enss

Pistol Packin' Madams: True Stories of Notorious Women of the Old West

Buffalo Gals: Women of Buffalo Bill's Wild West Show

The Doctor Wore Petticoats: Women Physicians of the Old West

How the West Was Worn: Bustles and Buckskins on the Wild Frontier

Hearts West: True Stories of Mail-Order Brides on the Frontier

A Beautiful Mine: Women Prospectors of the Old West

Frontier Teachers: Stories of Heroic Women of the Old West

The Lady Was a Gambler: True Stories of Notorious Women of the Old West

Outlaw Tales of California: True Stories of the Golden State's Most Infamous Crooks, Culprits, and Cutthroats

Tales Behind the Tombstones: The Deaths and Burials of the Old West's Most Nefarious Outlaws, Notorious Women, and Celebrated Lawmen

WITH JOANN CHARTIER

With Great Hope: Women of the California Gold Rush

Love Untamed: Romances of the Old West

Gilded Girls: Women Entertainers of the Old West

She Wore a Yellow Ribbon: Women Soldiers and Patriots of the Western Frontier

WITH HOWARD KAZANJIAN

The Young Duke: The Early Life of John Wayne

Happy Trails: A Pictorial Celebration of the Life and Times of Roy Rogers and Dale Evans

The Cowboy and the Señorita: A Biography of Roy Rogers and Dale Evans

Thunder over the Prairie: The True Story of a Murder and a Manhunt by the Greatest Posse of All Time

Sam Sixkiller: Cherokee Frontier Lawman

LOVE LESSONS
FROM THE OLD WEST

Wisdom from Wild Women

Chris Enss

Foreword by Brenda Novak

TWODOT®

GUILFORD, CONNECTICUT
HELENA, MONTANA
AN IMPRINT OF GLOBE PEQUOT PRESS

A · TWODOT® · BOOK

Text design/layout: Lisa Reneson
Project editor: Lauren Brancato

Library of Congress Cataloging-in-Publication Data

Enss, Chris, 1961-
Love lessons from the old West : wisdom from wild women / Chris Enss ; foreword by Brenda Novak.
   pages cm
 ISBN 978-0-7627-7400-5 (pbk.)
1. Courtship—West (U.S.)—History—19th century. 2. Women—West (U.S.)—Biography. 3. West (U.S.)—Social life and customs—19th century. 4. West (U.S.)—History—1848-1890. I. Title.
 HQ801.A2E57 2014
 306.73'409034—dc23
                              2013015027

Printed in the United States of America

10 9 8 7 6 5 4 3 2 1

For George

Contents

Foreword by *New York Times* Bestselling Author Brenda Novak, ix

Acknowledgments, xi

Introduction, xiii

Agnes Lake: Love and the Pistolero 1

Etta Place: Love and the Outlaw 13

Emma Walter: Love and the Pugilist 21

Lotta Crabtree: Love and the Matriarch. 35

Maria Josefa Jaramillo: Love and the Explorer. 49

Luzena Stanley Wilson: Love and the Gold Miner 63

Zoe Agnes Stratton: Love and the Lawman. 77

Calamity Jane: Love and the Legend 87

Geronimo's Wives: Love and the Indian Chief 101

Eleanora Dumont: Love and the Journalist 111

Notes, 119

Bibliography, 140

About the Author, 147

FOREWORD

The Old West.

Those three words conjure images of dirt trails, majestic horses, and a way of life that after so much time feels worlds away. But there is a unifying force that ties us inexplicably to our past: the undying power of love. Love affects us all—in what we do, what we think, and how we live our lives. It is as vital to us as the water we drink—and it was to the women in the West.

This far removed from a time when life was shorter and, in some ways, simpler (though not easier!), movies and TV often give an inaccurate, romanticized view of how people existed, especially the women. Most usually, the Old West is depicted by stereotypes—the gunslinger coming to town for revenge, the door-splitting saloon fight, prostitutes floating around a card room with a piano playing in the background. It's easy to forget that most of the people who populated the western region of our country were not so different from us.

Chris Enss's book, *Love Lessons from the Old West,* is a vivid reminder of our similarities. Every woman featured in this collection experienced love differently, and yet it enriched the women's lives in ways that transcend their deaths. Decades later we connect these women to the men who owned their hearts. Whether separated by circumstance, lifestyle, or death, these women prove that love, no matter how short a time you have it, changes you forever. I thank Chris for reminding me, and all those who read these stories, that no matter who we are or when we live, in the end, love is all that matters.

— Brenda Novak, *New York Times* bestselling
author of the Whiskey Creek series

ACKNOWLEDGMENTS

The idea for a book on this subject has always been something that has interested me. I could have used such a book on love lessons when I was in high school. I would have been particularly interested in the chapter about Calamity Jane. Like Calamity, I, too, was infatuated with a well-known person. It was the most remote of chances, I know, but I thought if I dressed and acted like "one of the guys" he might notice my talent and want to marry me. That's the way I thought Calamity Jane got Wild Bill Hickok's attention. Sadly for me, George Brett, third baseman for the Kansas City Royals, wasn't hanging around a ball field waiting for the lone girl on the baseball team to announce her undying devotion to him. The age difference alone would have made such a union illegal—I was thirteen, and Brett was twenty-one. That fact was of complete indifference to me.

Brett went on to set many major league baseball records, got married (not to me), had three children, and is co-owner of the Kansas City Royals. With my George Brett rookie baseball card tucked safely inside my wallet, I went on to write this book.

I'd like to take this opportunity to recognize those who inspired a need for *Love Lessons* . . . Johnny Bench, Cal Ripkin, and, of course, George Brett.

This, my twenty-fifth book on a western theme, has been written with devotion to all the makers of the West. Those brave pioneers who ventured into wild, uncharted territories in search of a better life. Without the help of the staff at the California State Library History Room, the men and women who run the Adams' Museum in Deadwood, the brilliant people at the Kansas Historical Society, the long-suffering librarians at the Madelyn Helling Library in Nevada County, California, and the courteous individuals at the Kit Carson Museum in Taos, New Mexico, I wouldn't have been able to acquire the historical documents necessary to complete the book.

Finally, to my patient editor, Erin Turner, and the staff of Globe Pequot Press, thank you for your expertise and dedication to the job. Erin, you are a wonder.

INTRODUCTION

This wasn't the first time Mary had turned her face when Jake bent to kiss her, but she caught the pained look on his face as he planted a light caress on her smooth cheek. All the other times she had withheld her lips for the same reason—jealousy. Not of another woman, but of their neighbor, Tom Dixon.

Mary tucked away a stray tendril of dark brown hair and picked up a shovel to turn the small stream of water from the spring down two dry rows of her garden. She puttered around in the mud, a slim, lithe figure in a gingham dress and beehive bonnet, while Jake saddled their horse and rode away.

She always thrilled a little when she watched him on a horse. He might be a bit awkward on the ground, but, mounted, he was the handsomest man she knew. He was tall, with the broad shoulders and narrow hips of a cowman, and on a horse his legs didn't look too long. She could see the little ducktails of straw-colored hair at the back of his neck.

Jake was the kindest man she had ever known. There would have been a look of tenderness in her eyes, except that she was a practical woman who would stand no nonsense from herself.

There had been other quarrels about Tom Dixon, but none as stormy as the one this morning. Mary had lost, as usual. Jake was on his way to slap a mortgage on their livestock to buy Tom Dixon a plow. He would ride the two miles to Dixon's place, and he and Tom would ride the forty miles to Sacramento. Jake had left Mary's horse, Matilda, saddled in the barn on the chance that she might want to use her.

Mary had given Jake an ultimatum that morning. "I warn you, Jake, if you let Dixon have that money I'll leave you. A man who will gamble everything he owns to help somebody else isn't thinking much of his own family."

Jake had answered wearily, "I've told you why I can't let Tom down. There's no use going over it again."

She had come close to telling Jake that she had only married him for security. Though it was very nearly true, she was glad now that she hadn't lost her temper quite that much.

Mary had told Jake when she married him that she was too old for romantic notions, but was tired of the lonely life of a country school-teacher, and would welcome companionship and a good home.

"That's what I want, too, so we ought to get along," Jake had said.

They had had the good companionship. Jake was a busy rancher, and though he hadn't had too much schooling, he had read a lot. They liked the same books and magazines. He had bought her the piano she had always wanted, and though Mary knew that she was no great shakes as a musician, Jake always pretended she was a marvel. He had taken her to the town social dances, though he didn't care much about dancing himself.

It had pinched him financially to buy the new homestead. *But I've tried to reciprocate*, Mary thought. *I've made him a good home.* She was proud of her house; it was one of the nicest along the American River. Against her own fastidious instincts, she allowed the living room to look just disorderly enough for Jake to brag that his friends could drop in wearing working clothes, and feel at home.

She raised a garden and her flowers were the envy of every hard-working ranch woman in the neighborhood. She did her full share of the chores. And, what she knew was more important to Jake, she was always willing to drop her work and ride into the hills with him, whenever he could find the time to go hunting or fishing or picnicking.

In short, they had a good, sensible marriage, and it could continue to be that way if it were not for Tom Dixon. But if Jake thought so much of Dixon that he was willing to let their marriage go on the rocks, it would just have to go. Mary wasn't a woman to give up a principle.

She kicked off a pair of muddy boots outside the door of the home, and glanced into the mirror as she came in. She opened her mouth a little as she realized she was wearing what Jake always called her schoolmarm look. Her lips were drawn into a straight hard line.

Mary had been twenty-eight when she married Jake, who was seven years her senior. She was wise, she had thought, to marry a man old enough to have made his start, and who knew what he was doing. They were still young enough to have children, and the doctor told them there was no reason why they shouldn't, if they would just learn to be patient. Mary wanted to learn the valuable lesson of being patient because ultimately she loved Jake deeply and she knew, although she seldom allowed him to say it, that he was deeply in love with her.

This fictionalized tale of Mary and Jake illustrates the two very different reasons for marriage in the Old West: romance and convenience.

In letters between would-be marriage partners in the 1800s, we see people who may or may not love each other. But they would agree that there were other reasons to marry, such as children and temperament. Those were far more important.

Where love existed, it didn't prove to be the most reliable glue when it came to keeping marriages together on the frontier. In the mid-1800s, the increasingly voluntary, romantic nature of marriage, plus an increasingly mobile society, led to a new trend—divorce. The 1870 census found that more than sixty-five hundred marriages west of the Mississippi ended in divorce, a trend that became a political issue of the day.

The high divorce rate set off a moral panic. States tried, through legislation, to make it harder to get divorced and keep people married, but it didn't take. Newlyweds had to build a home in rough, uncharted wilderness surrounded by Native Americans who resented them being there, and extreme weather conditions that made it next to impossible to see a new homestead through to a point where it would make money. Floods, droughts, prairie fires, and tornados ravaged the land and took their toll on married couples trying to make their way.

All love stories—somewhere amidst the romantic picnic outings, heated late-night rendezvous, and sometimes tragic futures—have personal morals, even if some of the lovers contained in this book don't seem to have any professional morals. For example, the famed gun-fighter the Sundance Kid and his lover, Etta Place, had no problem taking money from banks and robbing miners of their payrolls, but never considered betraying one another.

Some relationships were temporary. Such was the case of Apache Indian Chief Geronimo and his wife, Alope. They had planned to spend a lifetime together but a senseless murder deprived Geronimo of his spouse. Her memory was all he had to keep him going.

There were plenty of bumps and hard-to-swallow love lessons along the road toward happily ever after for the ladies included in this book. Maria Josefa Jaramillo Carson learned that her husband, Kit Carson, would never be content with the ordinary life of a rancher. Their marriage lasted more than twenty years because Kit traveled the West expanding the nation's territories. Maria was alone for much of their married life but the pair was devoted to one another.

Among the other women contained in this volume with price-less love lessons to share is business owner Luzena Stanley Wilson, equestrian Agnes Lake Hickok, and juggler and entertainer Emma Masterson. Heartaches were valuable love lessons as well. The story of popular child actress Lotta Crabtree and western legend Calamity Jane serve as examples of that sad fact.

So, grab a pen and piece of paper and be ready to take notes, and keep the Kleenex close by in case you have to wipe away a tear. The chapters in this book provide insight into possible motives for why frontier men and women fell in love. Some of the chapters will bring a smile to your heart; others will break it into pieces. As one California prospector noted in his diary in 1855, "I'd endure just about anything to settle down with a good woman. She don't have to love me, least not at first. I only want a chance to show her I could be the finest blanket companion in the country."

Love Lessons Learned by Agnes Lake

Be a successful businesswoman. Western legends, such as
Wild Bill Hickok, found this attractive. According to the
cowboy slang of the day, "Hosses an' smart wimmen will
shore make a man go 'histling, provided he's still young
'nough to pucker."

Allow yourself to be a damsel in distress sometimes—
nothing was more appealing to an Old West lawman.
Bill's friends noted that once he spoke up for the Widow
Lake at the city council meeting, "a look, a smile, or a kind
word from her could win him."

Don't be overawed by his celebrity. Whereas most women
at that time might have been quick to marry the legend
and not the man, Agnes suggested she and Wild Bill get
to know one another better by writing letters. Talk of love
and marriage came after courtship by correspondence.

Know your way around a horse and respect the animal.
Agnes was a talented equestrian and confident in her
ability. She could ride like a man, but never forgot she was
a woman.

Be self-sufficient. The eleven-year age difference between
Agnes and Wild Bill was a plus. As an older woman she
wasn't interesting in competing for his attention on the
same level as others. She was emotionally stable.

AGNES LAKE

Love and the Pistolero

A dusty haze hung in the air over the Kansas cowtown called Hays City, making the August sun appear cloudy and more distant than usual. The dirt film hovering before the giant orb did little to decrease the intense heat searing down on the town's inhabitants. The main thoroughfare was crowded with people. Cowhands, farmers, and mothers with distracted children weaved their way around a line of wagon trains with red and white colored canvas tops. The name LAKE'S CIRCUS was sprawled in big letters across the side of the vehicles. In the near distance sat a spectacularly large, partially assembled tent. A crew of perspiring workers unloaded a wagon filled with supports for the massive tent and laid them next to the spot where they were going to be used. Curious onlookers hurried to the spot to get a better look at the imposing display.[1]

Agnes Lake, a short, plain-looking woman, forty years of age, dressed in an ornately decorated, deep burgundy taffeta gown, emerged from the lead wagon and marched into the nearest mercantile. She wore a worried expression and carried a letter in her hand.[2]

The merchandise in half of the store had been moved to another area to make room for a long table and rows of chairs. Four town councilmen sat behind the table. Each was well dressed and neatly groomed. One studied an ad for Lake's Circus posted in the Wichita, Kansas, newspaper the *Wichita Daily,* two passed a bottle of liquor back and

Agnes Thatcher Lake was fifty years old when she married Wild Bill Hickok on March 5, 1876.

forth, and one man busied himself filling his pipe with tobacco and lighting it. He lifted it to his mouth and drew on it hard. The glow from the excited bowl kicked on his eyes, which were tracking Agnes as she walked in and took a seat in the back row among several other people in the gallery.

As the flyer made its way back around to the first councilman, he acknowledged Bill Hickok seated in the front row of the gallery with a nod. Bill stood up and scanned the faces of the council. Hickok was an imposing figure, more than six feet tall. His hair was shoulder length and thick, and his neatly trimmed mustache drooped below his determined chin along both sides of his well-defined jawline.[3]

"I never made a speech in my life and I don't want to begin now," Bill told the council, "but I never went back on a woman, and I'm going to give you some plain talk. You fellows live so far outside of civilization that your hearts have dried up like small potatoes left out in the sun, and you can't of course know nothing about what's going on here east of the coyotes' range.[4]

"This circus that's advertised to show and furnish a little amusement for us heathens is owned by a woman, one whose pluck catches my sympathy every time. Her husband, Bill Lake, was murdered down in Granby, Missouri, by a cowardly villain named Joe Killian, on the 24th of August 1869. The brave little widow, after burying her husband, had to either sell out or go on the road with the circus, and circumstances advised her to carry the show. My opinion is that any woman capable to run a circus is a darn sight bigger curiosity in these parts than the leatherheads in this village ever heard of, and when I see so much pluck in a woman, I just feel like throwing in and helping her.[5]

"Now, if your fellows that run this town knowed [sic] how to appreciate a good thing for the place, instead of charging Mrs. Lake a license, you would vote an appropriation to pay her for coming out here to show

3

us heathens a first-class circus. If I've got any authority in Hays, Mrs. Lake isn't going to pay this town a cent of license for showing and if any man attempts to stop this show then just put it down that he's got me to fight. That's all I've got to say now, so drive on, and we'll see who pays the fiddler."[6]

According to the August 29, 1929, edition of the Anita, Iowa, newspaper the *Tribune,* when Bill concluded his "talk" on August 2, 1871, the council of four decided to reconsider its action and the license. The meeting quickly concluded once the announcement was made, and spectators in the gallery rushed to congratulate Bill on the outcome. Agnes left the mercantile without being able to express her appreciation. She sent for Bill later that day and asked that he meet her at the circus tent. Dressed in his finest and with hat in hand, he complied with her request. After Agnes had thanked Bill for what he had done, she introduced him to all the members of her troupe, including her teenage daughter Emma.[7]

The *Tribune* reported that after seeing the paraphernalia of the circus and shaking the hands of the performers, Bill turned to Agnes and smiled proudly. "Well, now, all this is fine enough, but do you know the greatest curiosity about this canvas is yourself," the legendary lawman told the circus owner. "I never saw a woman before that could run anything except a broom handle, and to find one managing like this is a bigger sight than California Joe when he was tackled by a panther down in the Wachitas. I used to think that women never amounted to much, outside of being mothers, and I guess I wouldn't give them that much credit, if I hadn't had one myself, and a good one, too. But I've changed my opinion now. For if I could hitch up with such a business girl I'd go in search of a person tomorrow."[8]

Although Agnes didn't fully understand Bill's somewhat rambling address, she saw beneath his rough exterior a kind and healing sympathy, and a brave heart willing to protect the weak.

Agnes Louise Messman was born on August 23, 1826, in Doehm, Alsace, France. Her mother died when she was four years old, and, shortly thereafter, her father took Agnes to America. The Messmans settled in Cincinnati, Ohio, when she was sixteen years old. As a child Agnes was an avid horseback rider. Her father helped mold her remarkable skill into a circus routine. In 1841, Agnes met a circus clown named William Lake Thatcher. He was a native New Yorker and used his connections to secure a job for Agnes with the circus he worked for, the Spaulding & Rogers Circus.[9]

In addition to her impressive equestrian abilities, she also performed daring feats of skill on a tight wire. The August 23, 1907, edition of the *New York Times* reported that she "made a higher ascent on a wire than any performer of her day in 1858." By 1859, she was billed the "queen of the high wire" and the most famous equestrienne the American circus had ever known.[10]

Although her father disapproved of William Thatcher Lake, because of his profession and the vagabond lifestyle that went with the job, Agnes married him anyway. The pair wed in Louisiana in August 1842. William dropped the name of Thatcher so his and his bride's names would fit on the advertisement for the circus. Billed as Bill and Agnes Lake, the couple worked for Spaulding and Rogers for more than ten years. During that time they saved much of the money they earned with the hopes of starting a circus of their own. Their dream was partially realized in 1860 when Lake formed a partnership with veteran circus man John Robinson. The show was known as the Robinson-Lake Circus. William and Agnes devoted six years to the venture, then moved on to their own production. During that time the pair had a daughter they named Emma.[11]

At the conclusion of the first season of the Lake Circus, Agnes had toured all of Europe in an equestrienne-inspired play entitled

Shortly before Wild Bill Hickok was shot and killed in August 1876 he wrote a letter to his wife expressing his undying love for her.

Mazeppa. Back in the states, Lake's troupe spent three years performing at various locations from Syracuse, New York, to Independence, Missouri. Thirty-five wagons transported the show from town to town. In Pontiac, Michigan, Agnes and William hired a young boy named McGinnis to assist one of their performers, Frederick Bailey. McGinnis demonstrated a great aptitude for business and according to a report in the September 3, 1907, edition of the *Cedar Rapids Evening Gazette,* the youngster "eventually took the name of Bailey." Agnes insisted that when the boy grew up he should be made general agent of the show. The *Gazette* noted that, "Mr. Lake protested, but his wife had her way." That boy was James A. Bailey of the great Barnum and Bailey shows.[12]

In mid-1869, the Lake Circus returned to Granby, Missouri, then traveled west as far as Abilene, Kansas. During the Lakes' stay at the location, William got into an altercation with a man named Jake Killian (some historical records spell the last name Gillen). The Cheyenne, Wyoming, newspaper, the *Cheyenne Daily Leader,* reported that Killian had snuck into the circus tent and was trying to see the show without paying. William confronted him; the two men argued, and William kicked Killian out of the tent. Killian was furious. He pulled a gun out of his pocket and shot William in the head, killing him instantly. According to a report in the January 22, 1907, edition of the Galveston, Texas, newspaper, the *Galveston News,* "Killian surrendered to the authorities after the circus had left. . . . He had been a Union soldier, a man of ill-repute, it must be said, and in those days a very bad element controlled matters in Newtown County where the tragedy occurred."[13]

Agnes halted the show long enough to bury her husband and get her financial affairs in order. She then reassembled the circus troupe and continued on with a series of scheduled performances. The *Galveston News* article notes that Agnes never faltered in her duties. "Mr. Lake is dead," she reiterated to her employees after William's funeral. "In the future I intend to run the Lake Circus. If any of you think me incapable, all I ask is that you give me two weeks' notice and I shall try to fill your places.... I am determined to keep this show on the road, and I shall succeed."[14]

Lake Circus did well under Agnes's direction. She proved not only to be a talented performer but also a smart businesswoman. By 1872 she had earned a substantial amount touring and decided to sell the show to a competitor. She used the funds from the sale to invest in a lithograph business in Cincinnati. According to the August 23, 1907, edition of the *New York Times*, a serious economic downturn brought on by the drop in demand for silver plunged the United States and Europe into a major depression. Agnes lost everything and was forced to return to the circus.[15]

Bill Hickok, who was quite taken with the fearless proprietor of Lake Circus, wrote Agnes to express his concern for her well-being and share with her what was happening in his life since they last saw one another in Kansas. Agnes never failed to respond to his letters. For a short time they were both in the entertainment industry. Buffalo Bill Cody, the famous Pony Express rider, Indian scout, and showman, persuaded Bill to join a Wild West show he organized in 1873. Bill was one of the stars of the play entitled "Scouts of the Plains."[16]

In 1874, Agnes and Bill's paths converged in Rochester, New York. Bill was there with the Buffalo Bill Cody western show, and Agnes was in the city working for the Great Eastern Circus. According to the Des Moines, Iowa, newspaper, the *Tribune*, dated August 29, 1929, it was during this time that Bill told Agnes he was in love with her and asked her to marry him. Until Emma was grown and settled into a profession or married, Agnes did not feel she could commit to his proposal. It wasn't until Emma married in 1875 in Cincinnati that the chance presented itself for Bill and Agnes to see one another again. This time the two were in Cheyenne, Wyoming.[17]

Bill was making final arrangements to travel to the Black Hills of Dakota to search for gold. Agnes was in town visiting relatives. When Bill learned she was in Cheyenne, he hurried to see her. "Wild Bill then renewed his suit," the *Tribune* article noted, "and pressed his claims with such persistency that the engagement was perfected and arrangements concluded for the wedding, which it was agreed would take place on the following day."[18]

Several intimate friends of Bill's were surprised to receive invitations on the morning of March 5, 1876, to witness the wedding ceremony of J. B. Hickok (Wild Bill) and Mrs. Agnes Lake Thatcher on the afternoon of the same day. They all responded favorably, and when the couple stood up it was before an audience numbering about twenty persons.[19]

Reverend W. F. Warren, a Methodist minister, performed the service at the home of Agnes's relative L. S. Moyer, and after receiving many congratulations the couple took the evening train east to Saint Louis for their honeymoon. From Saint Louis the newlyweds made their way to Cincinnati, Ohio, where numerous friends and family members of Agnes's lived, including her daughter, son-in-law, and grandson.[20]

Less than two months after the couple were married, Bill departed for South Dakota. The discovery of gold in the Black Hills by Horatio Ross in 1874 had prompted a mad rush to the region, and nothing could keep Bill from his plan to travel there and find a rich claim of his own. Agnes chose to stay behind in Cincinnati. When she waved goodbye to her husband the day he left, she had no way of knowing it would be the last time she would see him alive.[21]

When Bill arrived at the mining camp town of Deadwood during the summer of 1876, it was teeming with illegal activity. Robbery, murder, and gunplay were commonplace. Law-abiding residents realized that in order for Deadwood to become inhabitable for everyone, some form of organized government would have to be established. An organization dedicated to bringing about law and order was gradually coming together. Bill was both admired and feared. His reputation for upholding the law was well known. Rumors circulated that he was to be appointed chief of police. His enemies heard the rumor and warned Bill against taking the job if offered and suggested strongly that he leave the area. Bill could not be threatened. He neither encouraged nor discouraged such talk, but went about working several gold claims he was developing.[22]

On July 17, 1876, Bill wrote his wife to let her know how the venture was going. "My own darling wife, Agnes," the correspondence began. "I have but a few moments left before this letter starts. I never was so well in my life, but you would laugh to see me now. Just got in from prospecting, will go again tomorrow, but god nowse [sic] when it will start. My friend will take this to Cheyenne where he lives. I don't expect to hear from you but it is all the same. I no [sic] my Agnes and only live to love her. Never mind, Pet, we will have a home yet, then we will be so happy. I am almost shure [sic] I will do well. The man is hurrying me. Goodby [sic], Dear Wife. Love to Emma. J. B. Hickok Wild Bill."[23]

On the afternoon of August 2, 1876, Bill was engaged in a friendly game of poker in the Number 10 Saloon. According to the August 2, 1876, edition of the Deadwood newspaper, the *Black Hills Pioneer,* the men in the game with him were laughing and joking as they played, but Bill was uneasy and worried. He sat with his back to the door, "a position so absolutely contrary to the caution that governed his alert and watchful habit that all his time-trained instincts were in violent rebellion." Several times he asked to change places with the others, but they refused and teased him about his nervousness.[24]

Sometime during the game, Jack "Broken Nose" McCall, a former buffalo hunter, entered the saloon and noiselessly walked toward Bill. No one paid any attention to him until he pulled a .45 caliber six-shooter and shot Bill in the head. "Damn you! Take that!" McCall yelled as the gun went off. McCall had been hired to kill Bill by a contingent of desperados who feared Bill would become marshal and bring their illegal activities to an end. The bullet perforated the back of Bill's skull, exited the front, and lodged into the arm of the poker player sitting opposite Bill. McCall fled the scene but was quickly apprehended.[25]

Agnes was with her daughter in Ohio when she received the news that Bill had been murdered. Bill Hickok was laid to rest in the Ingleside area of Deadwood, the site of the town's first Boothill. According to the August 29, 1929, edition of the Anita, Iowa, newspaper, the *Tribune*, among Bill's personal effects was a note he had written to Agnes dated August 1, 1876. "Agnes, darling: If such should be that we never meet again, while firing my last shot, I will greatly breathe the name of my wife, even for my enemies, I will make the plunge and try to swim to the other shore."[26]

On March 1, 1877, Jack McCall was tried and convicted for the murder of Bill Hickok. He was hanged and his body buried at the Sacred Heart Cemetery in Yankton, South Dakota.

In April 1877, Agnes had a monument erected in Bill Hickok's memory at his gravesite at Mount Moriah's Cemetery in Deadwood. She returned to work, performing with the John Robinson Circus until the fall of 1880. Agnes lived with her daughter and her family in Ohio and moved with them to Jersey City, New Jersey, in 1883.[27]

Agnes Lake Hickok died on August 22, 1907, at the home of her daughter and son-in-law. According to the August 23, 1907, edition of the *New York Times*, Agnes died of "general debility." "She had been an invalid for ten years previous to her death." Agnes was eighty years old when she passed away and was buried in Cincinnati, Ohio, next to her first husband.[28]

Love Lessons Learned by Etta Place

Know that your relationship is bound to have longevity problems when you're the paramour of an outlaw.

⊙

Share an interest in his work. According to various Old West newspapers, Etta participated in a number of holdups with Sundance and his partner in crime, Butch Cassidy.

⊙

Enjoy traveling. When Pinkerton detectives are chasing you night and day, you have to learn to love visiting many different places.

⊙

Keep your love life private. Etta never spoke out about her relationship with the Sundance Kid. Not only did that help keep their location secret, but it added to the mystery of the woman rumored to have been romantically involved with Butch Cassidy before she was involved with the Sundance Kid.

⊙

Be prepared to protect your man. Historians acknowledge that Etta was an excellent shot with a rifle, which came in handy when the Sundance Kid needed backup.

ETTA PLACE

Love and the Outlaw

A blazing hot sun shone through the branches of a few casadensis trees standing beside a crude wooden table in the patio of a small café in the town of San Vicente in Bolivia. The two men and one woman at the table pulled the chairs they were sitting on into the limited shade offered by the thin limbs of the trees. The city around them was noisy and crowded with people, some of whom were loud and nearly shouting their conversation to those with them as they made their way from one shop to another. Wagons without springs pulled by half-wild horses passed by, and the rattle of the wheels over the rocks and gravel added to the commotion.[1]

Robert LeRoy Parker, better known as Butch Cassidy, leaned forward in his chair in order for his friends to hear him over the racket in the street. Harry Longabaugh, also known as the Sundance Kid, and his paramour, Etta Place, leaned in closely to listen. Butch was regaling the pair with stories of the South American riches yet to be had by those willing to take them. Bolivia's plateaus were filled with silver, gold, copper, and oil. Butch's plan was to steal as much as they could of the income made by the people who mined or drilled for the resources there.[2]

Having spent much of their lives in the United States holding up trains and robbing banks, Butch and the Sundance Kid considered absconding with mining companies' payroll shipments to be a natural course of events. Butch reasoned that law enforcement in Bolivia was lacking and their chances of getting away with the crime great. His point had been proven many times in the six years the outlaws had been in South America. Since arriving in Bolivia in 1902, the trio had robbed numerous banks and intercepted one mule train after another carrying gold and paper money.[3]

After migrating to the land-locked city, Butch, Sundance, and Etta discussed another heist. A mule train rumored to be transporting a rich payroll was going to be in the area. It traveled a little-known route outside of San Vicente. Butch had a plan to overtake the train and meet back at the café shortly after the job was done. His cohorts in crime thought the idea had promise and were enthusiastic about the opportunity.

Twenty-eight-year-old Etta smiled happily at her two companions as the conversation strayed from the execution of the job to the large amount they had stolen. As the cheerful three laughed and reminisced about their crime wave, several members of the Bolivian Army sur-rounded the area. A gun suddenly fired, and a bullet almost took Butch's head off. The two men quickly dove under the table. Sundance pulled Etta down with him. Bullets ricocheted around them as they surveyed the scene looking for a place to take cover.[4]

Crouching low, Butch led his cohorts inside the tiny, vacant café. Sundance dared to look out an open window and spotted the owner of the establishment talking to the police. Another series of bullets smacked into the walls above the three. The outlaws fired their own weapons indiscriminately into the collection of law enforcement offi-cers that had gathered. For more than a day, Butch, Sundance, and Etta fought being overtaken by authorities. Various accounts about the exchange between the bandits and police, from the July 7, 1908, edi-tion of the *Washington Post* to the December 19, 1917, edition of the *San Antonio Light* newspapers, reported that the battle ended with the deaths of the outlaws in the spring of 1908.[5]

Etta was reportedly killed instantly by a bullet to the chest, and the Sundance Kid was critically wounded. Butch was shot several times, and, rather than allow himself and Sundance to be captured, he killed his dying friend, then turned the gun on himself. Bolivian soldiers claim they found Sundance lying next to Etta. She was dressed in cowboy clothes, and a gold watch from a New York jewelry store was pinned on her blood-smeared, flannel shirt.[6]

Historians and researchers debate the account of the final demise of Butch Cassidy, the Sundance Kid, and Etta Place. According to the September 18, 1920, edition of the *Seattle Post Intelligencer*, "It's likely no one will ever know what truly became of Cassidy and the Kid, but Etta is most certainly still alive." Calling her a "master criminal," the report contends she had been seen in Paris and Monte Carlo in the fall of 1915.[7]

Pinkerton Agency files (a detective agency established in 1850 that pursued Butch, Sundance, and the gang they ran with known as the Wild Bunch at the behest of the Union Pacific Railroad Company) described Etta as having "classic good looks, approximately 5'4" to 5'5" in height, weighing between one hundred ten pounds and one hundred fifteen pounds, with a medium build, reddish-brown hair, and cold gray eyes." Her date and place of birth are unknown, but the overall consensus was that she was from Utah or New York. She was well educated and an excellent horsewoman.[8]

With the exception of the Pinkerton Agency files, there is little concrete information about Etta. History writer Edward Kirby noted in his book *The Saga of Butch Cassidy and the Wild Bunch* that she was "truly the mystery woman of the Wild Bunch story."[9]

The Pinkerton Agency files, as well as an article in the *San Antonio Light* newspaper, note that Etta became acquainted with Butch Cassidy and the Sundance Kid in 1899 while working for Madam Fannie Porter at a brothel in San Antonio, Texas. Michael Rutter, an author

COURTESY LIBRARY OF CONGRESS

Etta Place and the Sundance Kid posed for this picture in New York shortly before traveling to South America.

who has written extensively on the life of Etta Place, speculates that she might have been romantically involved with Butch before entering into a relationship with the Sundance Kid. The same sources, as well as the Sundance Kid's family, report that Etta and Sundance married in December 1900.[10]

Some historical accounts record that she became the "outside man" for the gang Butch organized with her husband. She was the one who held the horses and remained on guard while they robbed and stole. "She bore the brunt of attack by aroused citizens and was always the last in the getaway," a *San Antonio Light* newspaper article read.[11]

There were dangerous desperados in the gang, men like Harvey Logan, alias Kid Curry, and Harry Tracy, whose names were synonymous in certain parts of the country with robbery, cattle stealing, and gunfighting. The gang had its headquarters in Grand Encampment, Wyoming, and rode hundreds of miles to strike for wealth in unsuspecting places. Montana, Wyoming, Texas, Arizona, and Nevada all suffered at the hands of the Wild Bunch, and posses of skilled trackers and fighters rode themselves haggard looking for the thieves.

By mid-January 1901, the Wild Bunch had gone their separate ways, and with the exception of Butch, Sundance, and Etta, who traveled to Pennsylvania and New York together, gang members confined themselves to locales in the West. On February 1, 1901, Etta and Sundance posed together for a picture at DeYoung's Photography Studio in New York after having made a purchase at Tiffany Jewelers. Sundance bought Etta a gold lapel watch. On February 20, 1901, the husband and wife boarded a ship bound for Buenos Aires, Argentina; there they met up with Butch Cassidy, who had gone ahead of them to secure a ranch for the three to live and work in the town of Cholila.[12]

Shortly after the trio was reunited in South America, they opened a bank account with twelve thousand dollars in gold notes. According to the February 19, 1950, edition of the *American Weekly*, Butch told the Buenos Aires bank president that he and his friends were afraid of thieves. When Robert Pinkerton, head of the Pinkerton Agency, learned what the outlaws had done, he was outraged. "It shows how daring these people are," he wrote his brother in 1905. "We hunt them in the mountains and the wilderness and they are in the midst of society . . ."[13]

From March 1901 to June 1904, Etta made several trips back to the states to visit her family. According to the Pinkerton Agency file, Sundance periodically accompanied her. The couple was spotted in Saint Louis, Missouri, at the World's Fair in 1904. The Pinkerton Agency had received word the pair was in the area and began tracking them. Etta and Sundance made it back to Argentina without interference from any law enforcement agency.[14]

Life on the ranch in Cholila proved to be too mundane for Butch, Etta, and Sundance. Reminiscing about their past adventures drove the former gang members back to their old habits. They robbed an English bank in the town of Patagonia, then rode into Chile where they committed a number of other daring robberies.

Their coffers filled with money again, the outlaws returned to Argentina and boldly went into Buenos Aires, had their picture taken, and then sailed away to Europe, going to Paris where they bought an assortment of clothing. Etta had her clothes tailored and adorned herself with expensive jewelry. The three visited museums, ate fine food, and attended the opera. They traveled to Monte Carlo, took up residence on the Riviera, and generally lived an easy life for a while.[15]

When the political climate in the region began to change and rumors surfaced that the Pinkerton Agency had picked up a lead on their whereabouts, the three felt it was best to leave the country. They disappeared in the night just as easily as they had done many times before. Pinkerton detectives raided the villa where the trio had been living, but found nothing that gave them a clue as to where the desperados were headed.

According to the *San Antonio Light* newspaper, three outlaws matching the description of Etta and her male cohorts were spotted at Cape Horn in early 1907. Although she was dressed in men's clothing, there seemed to be no question from the witnesses who noticed the woman that it was Etta. Law enforcement was lax in the region, and the bandits again got away.[16]

Butch Cassidy's sister, Lulu Parker Betensen, told reporters from the *Los Angeles Times* on April 7, 1970, that her brother and Etta were not killed by the Bolivian Army. "He visited me years after his reputed death," she shared. "We heard from him from time to time through the years until he died. It's my secret where he's buried." According to Lulu, Etta returned to America long before Butch and Sundance fought it out with the South American police. She did not know what became of the Sundance Kid, but Lulu believed Etta settled in Denver and taught school.[17]

Author and historian Richard Selcer wrote in his book *Hell's Half Acre* that Etta could very well have traveled to Denver with her husband. Selcer's research suggests she might have been suffering from acute appendicitis and needed emergency surgery. Selcer and other historians theorize that the romantic end of Etta's life with the Sundance Kid came when he escorted her to a Denver hospital and left her there. He rode away to escape the possibility of being caught by the Pinkerton men, and the couple never saw one another again. Another account formulated by research done by journalist Jim Dullenty indicates that Etta moved to Marion, Oregon, after hearing news that Sundance had been killed in Bolivia. She remarried and moved to Paraguay.[18]

An article in the December 26, 1917, edition of the *San Antonio Light* newspaper reported that Etta Place died on December 15, 1917. Because the news could not be confirmed, police doubted the bandit had indeed passed away. They believed the story was circulated to conceal her identity. "She wanted to avoid capture," New York law enforcement officials told the press. Some historians report that "Etta was supposedly killed by an unknown assailant."[19]

When and where Etta Place lived out the remainder of her life once the key leaders of the Wild Bunch were no more will probably always be left to conjecture. Historical documents do show that Etta and Sundance were dedicated to one another and that she was undeniably the "Queen of the Wild Bunch."[20]

Love Lessons Learned by Emma Walter

Stand out. With so many women vying for the attention of the famous gunfighter, you have to. And what better way to stand out than to have your name on a theater marquee . . . as a juggler?

Be adventurous. Not many women would consider crashing a sporting event just to be near the man they love. Emma did and her affectionate act was appreciated by the western legend.

Help him get what he wants. Although Bat was famous as a lawman, Emma learned that he was most happy writing about sports, particularly boxing matches, and helped persuade him to make that his life's work.

Understand what goes along with fame. Throughout their married life, Bat Masterson would be approached by dime novel readers, fans of the Old West, and fledgling gunfighters; Emma would have to learn to be patient while he engaged his fans and story writers.

Don't be afraid to go against the law to hold on to the man you love. Emma married Bat long before her divorce to her first husband was finalized. You can't let bigamy stand in the way of holding on to a man like Bat Masterson.

EMMA WALTER

Love and the Pugilist

The Olympic Club Amphitheatre in New Orleans was filled to over-flowing on January 14, 1891. Among the enthusiastic crowd that had converged on the scene was Bat Masterson, the charming, always well-dressed, part-time lawman, pugilist, and sportswriter. He sat closely to a twenty-four-square-foot boxing ring in the center of a massive room, under a bank of bright lights that surrounded the arena. Box holders and general ticket holders eager to see the fight between Jack Dempsey and Bob Fitzsimmons filtered through the main gate and quickly hurried to their assigned places. Security guards were stationed at several other entrances to the room keeping determined boxing fans from sneaking into the event without paying and barring entrance to any female who had a desire to see the highly publicized match.[1]

A competent announcer squeezed between the ropes carrying a speaking trumpet (predecessor of the megaphone) and positioned himself in the center of the canvas ring. In a clear, bold voice he introduced boxer Jack Dempsey to the more than four thousand spectators awaiting the action. Dempsey was escorted to the arena by his coach and his coach's assistant. The twenty-eight-year-old boxer wore a determined expression. Fitzsimmons, also twenty-eight, looked just as resolute about the work to come when he appeared and was led to the ring. Cheers erupted for the pair. At the request of the referee both men shook hands and at the appropriate time began to fight.[2]

21

MRS. "BAT" MASTERSON.

Emma Walter Masterson married the famous gunfighter Bat Masterson in 1873.

The audience and amphitheatre staff were transfixed by the action. Fans jumped to their feet at times and shouted instructions to the boxer they wanted to be victorious. A pair of guards at a side entrance of the club was so focused on the boxers in the ring they scarcely noticed the medium-height man pass by them wearing a derby hat, black coat, and tan trousers. The dark-haired, mustached gentleman kept an even pace with two men flanked on either side of him who appeared to be his friends. They exchanged a few pleasant words with one another as they made their way toward the ring. When the three reached the spot where Bat Masterson was seated, they stopped and the dapper man wearing the derby hat leaned down to speak to the western legend. Bat looked away from the boxing match a bit surprised and smiled.[3]

A reporter sitting nearby witnessed the scene, jumped to his feet, and pointed at the person wearing the derby hat. "That's a woman!" he shouted incredulously. Uniformed guards quickly swarmed the scene, grabbed the imposter's arms, and swiftly ushered her toward the exit of the building. In the commotion the derby hat fell off and a curly mop of brunette hair tumbled out from under the hat. It was indeed a woman. It was Emma Walter Moulton, world renowned juggler and sometimes professional foot racer. She was there because her lover, Bat Masterson, was there, and she didn't want to be away from him.[4]

According to a newspaper account of the incident in the January 17, 1891, edition of *New York Clipper*, "The woman was greatly embarrassed, but she withstood the ordeal wonderfully well. She was placed in a streetcar and taken to the 5th Precinct Station. Her name was Emma Walters [*sic*] and her age was thirty years." Emma was jailed for violating a city ordinance that made it illegal for women to attend public sporting events. After several hours of being locked up, she was bailed out of jail by Jake Kilrain, one of Bat Masterson's friends from Denver.[5]

Emma Matilda Walter, the woman who dared venture into the exclusive territory of the opposite sex to be near the infamous western figure, was born in Roxborough, West Philadelphia, on July 10, 1858. Her father, John, drove freight wagons for a living and continued in that line of work for the Union Army during the Civil War. He died of typhoid fever in 1862. Catherine, Emma's mother, was unable to

"BAT" MASTERSON.

Bartholomew "Bat" Masterson was a figure of the American Old West known as a buffalo hunter, US Marshal and Army scout, avid fisherman, gambler, frontier lawman, and sports editor and columnist for the New York Morning Telegraph.

support herself, Emma, and Emma's younger sister, so they went to live with Catherine's brother, William Banton, in Montgomery County, Pennsylvania. When William could no longer afford to care for them, the three moved to West Philadelphia to live with Catherine's mother.[6]

In 1872, Emma made the acquaintance of Edwin Winford Moulton, a twenty-five-year-old Minnesota native and professional athlete who had made a name for himself as a foot racer. He often appeared at state fairs where overconfident men would bet money on themselves that they could run faster and farther than Edwin. Edwin seldom, if ever, lost. In 1868, he boldly challenged any runner in the Northeast to compete against him. While traveling through Pennsylvania in October 1872, in search of a worthy opponent to answer the call, he met Emma. The two quickly fell in love and were married on January 13, 1873, at the Asbury Methodist Episcopal Church in Philadelphia.[7]

For a short time after Emma and Edwin were wed, Edwin continued to travel the fair circuit. Time and time again he proved himself to be the fastest runner, earning a modest amount of cash in the process. He was listed as one of the top three sprinters in the country in February 1874. Although he was pleased with the recognition, Edwin did not feel his income was compensatory to the work and travel he had to do. He missed his bride but knew he could not support them both on the road. In an attempt to generate more work, he developed a plan to incorporate Emma into the business.[8]

In September 1874, Edwin announced that he and Emma would be racing against one another in the one-hundred-yard dash at a series of scheduled fairs. Newspapers and magazines containing articles about the events captivated the public's attention. Audiences turned out in droves to see the woman who would dare match her skills with a sprinter who had won more than three hundred races. The popularity of the unusual challenge was evident in the increased ticket sales. Not only did the Moultons benefit monetarily from the race, but they also sold numerous photographs of themselves in their running uniforms. Emma was thrust into the limelight with her husband, and she reveled in the attention.[9]

In October 1875, the Moultons raced in front of a large crowd at the North Hampton, Massachusetts, county fair; so many people had gathered at the site of the happening that Emma and Edwin could barely move. When they finally made it through the throngs of spectators and the race commenced, Emma beat Edwin by two feet. Edwin took advantage of his wife's accomplishment and growing popularity and announced he would offer a cash prize to any woman who raced against her and won. There is no record of anyone accepting the challenge.[10]

For the next three years the pair toured the country entertaining fairgoers with their speed and agility. At some time during this period, Emma learned how to juggle, and she became proficient in Indian club swinging, using bowling-pin shaped clubs once used primarily for exercising.[11] Her talent was recognized by a theatrical agent who encouraged her to pursue a stage career. Emma took his advice and developed a few routines—including a trick called the "hurry" in which all the clubs are passed from hand to hand in lightning-speed succession. The style of Indian clubs Emma used weighed two pounds each and were six and a half inches long.[12]

According to an informational pamphlet about the clubs published in 1886 by the *Montgomery Ward Co.*, club swinging was considered a type of gymnastics relegated specifically to men. The author of the pamphlet believed women lacked the upper body strength necessary to keep the clubs moving. Emma was the exception. Theater owners in Boston, Chicago, and Providence, Rhode Island, hired her to appear on stage with her act. She was a major draw. By 1877 Emma was known as the "Queen of Clubs."[13]

Edwin refused to deviate from the ongoing schedule he had set for himself with various fair organizers to be with Emma, and their relationship began to falter. The couple became even more estranged in

August 1878 when Emma joined celebrated pantomimist Tony Denier's Humpty Dumpty theatrical troupe. Denier's Humpty Dumpty troupe consisted of twenty-five different acts from performing elephants to gymnasts. Emma, billed as the "Champion of All Lady Club-Swingers," committed to play venues from New Jersey to Utah.[14]

Emma and Edwin rarely saw one another during the 1878–1879 theatrical seasons. She began spending a great deal of time with acrobat Frank Clifton. Frank performed with his brother James, and both were members of Denier's troupe. Emma was frequently seen in public with Frank, but her involvement with the acrobat went largely unnoticed by newspapers until the company's last show, which was set in Chicago.[15] "The Champion Club-Swinger Emma Moulton is charged with running away from her husband, E. W. Moulton, to join Frank Clifton, a horizontal-bar athlete . . . ," an article in the August 17, 1879, edition of the *Chicago Daily Tribune* reported. "Clifton was last evening arrested upon a warrant charging him with adultery, but Mrs. Moulton could not be found. The injured husband is willing not to prosecute if Emma will return to her mother's home at Philadelphia and quit forever the variety business, which he always objected to her entering. Clifton pleads not guilty, of course, but Moulton says he can prove that they roomed together for a week at No. 409 W. Madison Street."[16]

Days after the news that Emma and Frank were romantically involved, the two decided to go their separate ways. Neither believed the affair could survive given the scandal that erupted. After being released from jail, Frank left Chicago and found work with another troupe located on the East Coast. Emma and Edwin reconciled and returned to life on the road. Edwin was no longer running foot races. He had ventured into the business of training athletes. His clients included sprinters, wrestlers, boxers, and bicyclists. Emma continued with her juggling act and added singing to her repertoire as well.[17]

According to the April 21, 1884, edition of *Rocky Mountain News*, the Moultons had journeyed west and Emma was appearing at various clubs in Denver. Between 1883 and 1887, Emma and Edwin traveled from their home base in Minneapolis to theaters and fairs beyond the Mississippi. Emma received glowing notices and, consequently, more requests to perform. In 1888 Emma accepted an extended engagement to appear in Denver, Colorado. Edwin, who was now coaching outstanding runners like Al Tharnish, the world's fastest human, and future Olympian Alvin Kraenzlein, objected to Emma spending so much time away from him. An altercation the two had on March 15, 1889, about that issue made the *Rocky Mountain News*. The article contained harsh accusations about both Edwin and Emma.[18]

> *Edwin Moulton was arrested last night at the corner of 18th and Larimer Streets after a hard fight. Moulton is a foot racer by profession, and under that guise he has duped many men out of hundreds of dollars. . . . Last fall Moulton's wife, who is engaged in one of the variety theatres, ran away with a negro minstrel named Shehan, to Los Angeles. Moulton obtained a letter of introduction to the chief of police in that place, went there and, after locating his better half, fleeced the head of the police department out of $50 and departed for home. He has been in Denver for some time, and when times are dull and "suckers" few, he spends his time gambling. He takes the proceeds of his wife's disreputable earnings and makes her life miserable generally.[19]*

Although nothing was made official until 1893, the Moultons' marriage did not survive. Edwin returned to Minnesota where he was hired by the University of Minnesota to be the trainer and head coach of the football team. Emma remained in Denver where she appeared on stage at Denver's Palace Variety Theatre and Gambling Parlor. The seven-hundred-fifty-seat performance hall and gambling facility was managed by celebrated former lawman Bat Masterson. Historians and biographers such as Robert DeArment believe Emma and Bat had been involved for years prior to Bat taking over the Palace; other scholars like Chris Penn (a contributing writer for *Wild West Magazine*) insist they met in March 1889, a month before Emma was hired to perform at the theater. The fact that the pair became lovers and eventually married is not disputed.[20]

Bat Masterson was four years older than Emma. Born Bartholomew Masterson in Canada in 1853, Bat had been employed in a number of professions prior to managing the Denver theater. He left home at the age of seventeen with his brother Ed and became a buffalo skinner in Kansas. He worked as a grader for the Atchinson, Topeka and Santa Fe Railroad; a scout for the army; and a buffalo hunter. Bat was an expert with a gun and on July 27, 1874, was the youngest of twenty-nine defenders at the Battle of Adobe Walls, a fight between buffalo hunters and the Plains Indians.[21]

On November 8, 1874, he was a participant in the renowned epic "Charge of the Wagon Brigade," when scouts located Cheyenne medicine man and chief Gray Beard's camp on McCleland Creek in Colorado. Lieutenant Frank Baldwin with the Sixth Cavalry attacked the camp, routed the Indians, and rescued two girls who had been held captive since September 11, 1874, when Gray Beard's band had massacred the rest of their family along the Smoky Trail in Kansas.[22]

It was during his experience as a scout that Bat killed a man to save his own life. It happened in Sweetwater, Texas, on January 25, 1875, at a dance hall. Bat and a friend, Virginia Riordan (also known as Molly Brennan), went to the dance hall after hours to have a snack. Sergeant Mel King, a member of the Fourth United States Cavalry, heard of this and became insanely jealous because he considered Molly to be his girl.[23]

Shortly after Bat and the woman had gone into the building and lit a small kerosene lamp, the drunken King walked through the doorway. Molly jumped in front of Bat and begged the soldier-gunslinger not to shoot. King fired point blank at the woman. The room was filled with her screams as well as with the stench of gunpowder and burned flesh. The bullet passed through Molly's abdomen and entered Bat's pelvic bone. As Molly fell on the floor dead, Bat fired his revolver and shot King through the heart.[24]

The shots aroused the saloonkeeper who rushed to the scene with some neighbors. The local doctor said that Bat would not live. His friends refused to accept the diagnosis. They took Bat to an army surgeon who removed the slug and continued to treat him. He recovered fully with no ill effect apart from a slight limp, which he carried for the remainder of his life.[25]

By the time Bat was well again, the Indian trouble had subsided and he was no longer needed as an army scout in the Panhandle country. He went to Dodge City, Kansas, where he became sheriff of Ford County. Not only did he distinguish himself as a law enforcement officer, leading posses in successful pursuits of train robbers, murderers, and horse thieves, but also as one of the owners of the Long Branch Saloon. He had a reputation as a shrewd businessman and possessed talent for gambling and worked on perfecting the art whenever he wasn't on duty. He enjoyed sporting events—horse racing, bear wrestling, and particularly boxing. He refereed several boxing matches and became a fine pugilist in the process.[26]

The summer of 1876 found Bat on his way to Deadwood, South Dakota, to try his luck searching for gold in the Black Hills. He never reached Deadwood, however; he stopped off at Cheyenne, Wyoming, where his gambling luck became so fantastic he decided to stay for a while. In the fall of 1876 he returned to Dodge City to help a friend in trouble. He took another turn as a law enforcement agent in the area, remaining in office as a US marshal until January 1880. He drifted into Colorado, Nebraska, and Arizona, involving himself in a variety of altercations with outlaws and gunfighters riding roughshod over the various territories. In between keeping the peace in different western locales, Bat traveled back to Dodge City time and time again. He had made lasting friends at the cattle town and was concerned for their well-being. In November 1884, he decided to start his own newspaper in Dodge City. He called it *Vox Populi*, but it didn't survive its first edition. Bat printed unflattering articles about political figures in the county, and the paper was not well received.[27]

By 1890 Bat was back in Colorado dealing faro at popular gambling halls in Denver until he took over management duties at the Palace Variety Theatre. Emma's song-dance-juggling act was a favorite with Palace audiences. Bat gave her top billing on the theater's marquee, and when the footlights were extinguished in the evenings the entertainer and manager would retire to the same hotel suite. According to author and researcher George G. Thompson, who acquired information about Bat from his brother Thomas, Emma and Bat were married on November 21, 1891. A record of the marriage has yet to be found, but divorce records do exist between Emma and Edwin Moulton. They show that the estranged couple's marriage was legally dissolved on November 9, 1893.[28]

Emma retired from the stage in 1892 and contented herself with being wife to Bat. She preferred the behind-the-scenes life filled with housework, bridge with friends, and reading.[29]

Bat eventually gave up his job at the Palace and went to Creede, Colorado, where he operated a gambling house and saloon. During his stay there he decided to become a promoter of horse races and boxing matches. Bat went broke backing boxers Charlie Mitchell and Bob Fitzsimmons in two separate bouts against James Corbet.

Bat traveled a great deal, unaccompanied by Emma more often than not. She missed him but was not insistent that he stay put. Likewise, Bat was aware that Emma enjoyed her independence. Their lifestyles suited them fine. According to the August 29, 1895, edition of the Glenwood, Iowa, newspaper, the *Mills County Tribune*, "Masterson is very happily married, and has an interesting family, his wife being a cultivated lady."[30]

At the turn of the century, the Mastersons were living in New York. Bat had accepted an offer from President Theodore Roosevelt to be the US marshal for the Southern District of New York. Emma and Bat both appreciated the job. Bat was home evenings, and, in contrast to the unpredictable earnings of sports promotions, the government salary was steady and substantial.

In 1903 Bat resigned from his post as US marshal and took a job as sports editor of New York's *Morning Telegraph* newspaper. Emma was proud of the opportunities that Bat was presented, but the East Coast climate was hard on her health. She suffered with asthma and epilepsy, a condition made worse by the area's damp weather. Colorado's weather was dry and the air crisp. Bat tried to persuade Emma they needed to return to the West, but she refused. She did not want him to sacrifice a job for which he was perfectly suited just for her.[31]

On Tuesday morning, October 25, 1921, shortly before noon, Bat strolled into the newspaper office to write his column. That afternoon he was found dead at his desk, slumped in his favorite chair, his last column clutched in his hand. The cause of death was a heart attack. He was sixty-six when he passed away. Emma was devastated. She laid her husband to rest at the Woodlawn Cemetery in New York. The inscription on his tombstone read "Loved By All."

Emma lived another eleven years and was faithful to Bat to the end. She died on July 12, 1932. Local newspapers carried a six-line obituary about her passing. "Mrs. Emma Masterson, widow of William Barclay 'Bat' Masterson, celebrated Western pioneer, was found dead in a New York hotel where she had been living three years," the Canadian newspaper the *Lethbridge Herald* notice read. "Emma was seventy-four years old."[32]

The couple had never had children. Their belongings were left to her sister. Emma was buried next to her beloved Bat.[33]

Love Lessons Learned
by Lotta Crabtree

Make sure your mother's managerial duties do not extend into your personal life if she's your theatrical manager.

Take time away from work and from family. Lotta worked constantly from the time she turned six years old until she retired at the age of forty-five. Any vacation was spent with her mother, brothers, or both. Any hope a potential suitor might have had for a romantic moment with Lotta was dashed by the ever-present Crabtrees.

Attend more parties hosted by Jack Crabtree. The parties Lotta's brother hosted were a favorite with Broadway celebrities, musicians, and champion athletes. The chances of meeting someone special without Mary Ann looking on were good.

Give yourself an allowance to spend any way you like. Mary Ann was instrumental in making sure Lotta's earnings were wisely invested, but the scrutiny she had over the funds limited Lotta's fun.

Don't put your career and your mother first or your love life will suffer.

LOTTA CRABTREE

Love and the Matriarch

In September 1884, six weary journalists spent three unusually hot and humid days loitering around the New York harbor waiting for the world famous entertainer Lotta Crabtree to arrive. Lotta was on her way to the city where she had perfected her career. The moment her steamship docked, the scribes rifled through their pockets for pencils and notepads. They scribbled Lotta's name across the tops of their notepads while anxiously waiting for her to appear. She had been away from the area for several years, performing on stages in New York, London, and Paris.[1]

Devoted fans, curious about what she would say when she stepped off the steamship *America* and looked around at the city that favored her, had gathered at the harbor. That her remarks would be voluminous, spirited, and to the point, no reporter or fan doubted. Journalists had been furnished with a little information about what she would say from her energetic manager, J. K. Tillotson. Tillotson had sent a short message to several newspaper editors across the country informing them that Lotta would make mention of her time abroad and address rumors that she had married in France. Reporters familiar with Lotta's mother, Mary Ann Crabtree, thought it highly unlikely the red-headed star would have been allowed to do such a thing, but they had to be sure.[2]

Mary Ann was the quintessential stage mother. She was dedicated to seeing that Lotta became the best, most beloved actress on any stage.

35

COURTESY OF THE CALIFORNIA STATE LIBRARY HISTORY ROOM

Lotta Mignon Crabtree began her career as the darling of the mining camps and ended as the toast of Broadway. She was loved by millions, but her mother kept her from ever being a wife.

Toward that effort she had halted every romantic overture young men had made toward her daughter. Falling in love and getting married could interfere with the success Lotta worked so long and hard to achieve.[3]

Lotta was among the men and women making their way down the gangplank when the steamship finally docked and the passengers disembarked. According to various newspaper accounts, the thirty-seven-year-old star "looked very unassuming and was clothed like a little English servant girl out for a Sunday, in a loose blue dress without a suspicion of crinoline and a meek little Quaker bonnet. The only feature about the little lady which suggested her profession was her extraordinary red hair."[4]

Lotta was greeted by a dozen or so lady fans that presented her with flowers and kissed her cheeks. The six weary reporters gathered around Lotta, and she looked up with surprise just as another woman was welcoming her with a kiss. "Miss Lotta," a scribe said, ambling forward, the September 4, 1884, edition of the *San Francisco Call* reported. "I'm a representative of the press come to interview you. These are my colleagues. We want to write up something you will like."

"I've nothing to say," Lotta told them coldly. "Nothing whatsoever. Good afternoon."[5]

"Miss Lotta," said another, "Mister Tillotson, your manager, wrote us letters about your arrival. Now, Miss Lotta, let us hear of your experiences. What of your recent nuptials?"

"Really," said Lotta, in a tone that was just as cold as her last comment. "I can't help what Mister Tillotson told you. I have nothing to say and no time to say it."[6]

For five years newspapers had erroneously reported that Lotta had exchanged vows with three different men. In December 1879, the *Daily Democrat* in Sedalia, Missouri, claimed she met and married a man named W. H. Smith, a manager of a San Francisco theater. In July 1883, the *Burlington Hawkeye* in Burlington, New Jersey, reported that she married an O. Edwin Huss, and an article in the October 5, 1883, newspaper the *Decatur Weekly Republican* in Decatur, Illinois, read that she had wed Bolton Hulme.[7]

A musician from London was among two men who claimed to have met and married Lotta during her European tour. Although one of the men, Charles F. Morrow from Manchester, had posted a notice in the *London Times* announcing that "he and Miss Crabtree were never wed," reporters persisted in asking about the incident.[8]

By September 1884, Lotta had grown tired of addressing the false reports and refused to dignify any more queries about such rumors with an answer.[9]

After the ordeal with the journalists at the ship's arrival in New York, Lotta was transported by carriage to the home she shared with her mother on Twenty-third Street. Her mother and manager then explained to Lotta that her treatment of the press was ill-advised. According to an article in the September 16, 1884, edition of the *New York Times*, "Lotta was seized with remorse at having neglected so good an opportunity to say something." She sent word to the journalists that she would be home that evening and would be glad to see them. The reporters went to the house at the appropriate time and again prepared themselves to interview Lotta.[10]

"Mrs. Crabtree, the lady to whom Lotta owes her existence and who also returned by the *America,* was found in the dining room," the *New York Times* article continued. "My daughter will be in very shortly," said Mrs. Crabtree, adding, by the way, that she was delighted to see them. "It is fifteen months come tomorrow since we left New York," she said. "Dear me, how time flies. You know Lotta went over to play a ten week's engagement and then protracted it to seven months. Isn't that extraordinary? The Londoners were delighted with her."[11]

At that moment Lotta entered the room, smiling prettily. She never once referred to the scene at the docks. She had a neat little stereotyped story of having taken London by storm and then left the poor metropolis to its fate. "I must confess," she said, "that the English people did not like 'Musette' [the musical in which she starred] at first. But they were delighted with 'Little Nell and the Marchioness' and 'Nitouche.' They swear they'll never have another Marchioness.

Isn't that sweet of them?" asked the little actress. "They're such an enthusiastic nation."[12]

"I only hope you'll do as well here, love," interposed Mrs. Crabtree. "Then you ought to be doubly delighted."

"Yes, ma," said Lotta. "I ought."

"The Prince of Wales came to see Lotta," Mrs. Crabtree continued. "He was delightfully kind and passed such a pleasant evening."

"Did he call at the house afterwards?" one of the journalists asked.

"Oh, no," said Lotta. "Let me try and recollect exactly what happened. I want to be precise."

"He said you were very clever," Mrs. Crabtree interjected.[13]

Lotta elaborated on her time in London and the various dinners she had the fortune of being invited to attend. She shared with the reporters that she was a guest of Queen Victoria and Lord and Lady Londesborough (British politician and diplomat). "Now," said Lotta in conclusion, "If only I do as well here as I did in Europe. I have a new play written for me by Ed Kidder called 'Dorothy Dent' I'll be starring in and . . ."

"Above all," interrupted Mrs. Crabtree, "I must say that Lotta made beautiful headway in England and mixed in lovely society."[14]

No further questions were posed about Lotta's marital status. The interview ended on a pleasant note. Mary Ann thanked the journalists for coming, Lotta waved graciously to them, and her mother and manager escorted her to her room.[15]

From the moment Lotta became the "Darling of the Mines" in 1853, her life both on and off the stage was the subject of much curiosity. Charlotte "Lotta" Mignon Crabtree was born in New York on November 7, 1847. She was the idol of hundreds of young men who only saw her as she dashed in and out of the theater. Her parents, John and Mary Ann Crabtree, ran a bookstore. John, a tall man who wore beaver hats, ignored the business and spent much of his time trying to find a shortcut to getting rich and enjoying "the good life," as he called it, in a saloon.[16] Mary Ann kept the shop afloat, occasionally bringing in money by working as an upholsterer. Her serious, responsible nature was reflected in her manner of dress. She always wore a one-piece, black taffeta, Princess-style frock. She knew almost immediately that she had made a mistake when she married John, but she was determined to stick it out. Her husband was less dedicated to making it work.[17]

John came down with gold fever in 1851 and decided to move west to find a fortune. Little did he know his daughter would soon be bringing in more gold than he could ever acquire panning or mining for the riches. Mary Ann followed her husband to California in 1852. John was supposed to meet his family in San Francisco, but, true to his character, he never showed up.[18]

Mary Ann found herself alone in a booming metropolis with no prospects and a child to care for. She sat down on the docks next to the ship that had brought her there to think about what to do. Her situation wasn't unique. Many wives and children were left stranded in the Gold Country by their husbands and fathers. Mary Ann stared down into the happy, smiling face of her daughter and realized she had to make the best of the circumstances. She appealed for help to a few people whom she had befriended on the ship. Mary Ann moved in with some of these generous new friends and tried to build a life for herself and her daughter.[19]

Theatrical shows were very popular in San Francisco. The various playhouses were always filled with bored miners looking to be amused. As the need for entertainment grew, more performers came to town daily. Variety shows sprung up overnight and featured acrobats, singers, and slapstick comedians. Child actors were held in particularly high regard because they reminded the miners of the sons and daughters they had left behind to search for gold.

Mary Ann loved the theater and took Lotta to see the shows as often as she could. Early on in her life, Mary Ann had wanted to be a performer, but she had abandoned that dream to get married. She watched the actors, singers, and dancers with great admiration and kept a close eye on how many people were in the audience. She noticed that the Forty-Niners were willing to pay handsomely to see the shows, and she wanted to get in on the act. It wasn't long before she became friends with a circle of the most popular actors of the nineteenth century. Her plan was to use them to transform her vibrant, talented, bubbly little girl into a star. Mary Ann enrolled Lotta in a dancing class and encouraged her daughter's acting aspirations.

John Crabtree finally contacted his wife in 1853 and begged for her forgiveness. He confessed that he had found nothing but a few flakes of gold while panning in the creek beds around Sutter's Mill. He pleaded with Mary Ann to join him in Grass Valley, California. He had it in his mind to run a boardinghouse for miners there. Mary Ann reluctantly agreed to follow her husband. She was less than impressed with the gold mining town when she arrived.

Grass Valley was no San Francisco. It had a population of only 3,500. Three hundred were women, and fifteen were school-age children. The town was rustic and lacked many of the opportunities she wanted Lotta to have. She helped John open their second-class, two-story boardinghouse on Main Street and enrolled Lotta in the only dancing school around. The classes were conducted in the annex of a tavern.[20]

Jared Reynolds was Lotta's dance instructor, and he was quite taken with her abilities. Many of the miners who stopped in the saloon for a drink gathered around to watch her twirl across the tiny stage. Tears would well up in their eyes as they thought of their own children. Half of California's foreign-born population was Irish in the 1850s. Jared knew this and made sure his pupil could dance jigs and reels—dances very popular in Ireland. One day, soon after she had mastered those dances, the dance instructor loaded Lotta in a buggy and, without asking her parents, took off for the gold fields.

It was the height of the California Gold Rush; the place was Rabbit Creek, and Lotta was six years old. She danced in the light of the candles, her red hair sparkling and her blue eyes flashing underneath the tall green hat she wore. Miners loved her act and tossed gold nuggets at her feet, starting a fortune that would eventually amount to more than $4 million when she died. When Lotta didn't return home after class that evening, Mary Ann and John were frantic. The Crabtrees' first child, Harriet, had died in infancy, and this naturally made them very protective of Lotta.[21]

After a few hours, Jared returned the child to her home with news that her dancing was a huge hit with the miners in the hills. He wanted to organize a musical troupe and escort Lotta around the gold fields with them. Mary Ann wasn't in the mood to hear his plan. She was furious with Jared for taking Lotta without permission and reprimanded him for his actions. John thought Jared's idea had promise, but Mary Ann refused to listen to him.

Just as Lotta was refining her skills with her instructors, John moved his family out of Grass Valley and headed north to Rabbit Creek (the same camp town to which Jared had taken Lotta to perform). After opening up another boardinghouse, John left his wife and two children to go on another gold search. Mary Ann was left to handle the business again. She resented cleaning up after unwashed, dirty miners. She knew Lotta was the answer to a better life.

During her stay in Rabbit Creek, Mary Ann met Mart Taylor, a musician and dancer who managed a saloon and crude theater where traveling players often appeared. Mary Ann convinced him to let Lotta perform for his customers. Lotta danced and sang a couple of sentimental ballads. She was a hit, and Mart Taylor quickly took her under his supervision.

Mart Taylor and Mary Ann quickly put together a company of musicians and set off to travel the various mining camps with their pint-sized gold mine. Lotta was well received wherever the troupe went, and she earned about thirteen dollars a night dancing and singing. Still unable to strike it rich, Lotta's father joined the troupe and toured with them for a time. He was amazed at the reaction his daughter got in the mining camps. She was greeted by thunderous applause followed by showers of coins and nuggets. He'd not seen that much gold in all the time he had been prospecting. Mary Ann knew Lotta's act could earn more money in big city theaters. This time it was Mary Ann who decided to move the family back to San Francisco.

Lotta performed at variety halls and amusement parks and became known as the "San Francisco Favorite." She was twelve and the sole supporter of her family, which now included two brothers.[22]

Mary Ann was in charge of every aspect of Lotta's career. She made her costumes, applied her makeup, booked her into the various performance halls, and made sure the schedule allowed for Lotta to take parts in plays at the better theaters in San Francisco. She handled all of Lotta's money as well, insisting on getting Lotta's share after the box office closed each night rather than waiting until the end of the week. She had a mortal fear of theater fires. A theater's gas footlights could, and often did, explode and cause a fire that would consume a building in a matter of minutes.

Lotta was devoted to her mother. Her high spirits and irrepressible good humor on stage reflected Mary Ann's boundless confidence in her. Mary Ann prevented Lotta from having any intimate contacts or lasting friends, however. She wanted her daughter to be totally dependent on her.

Under the watchful eye of Mary Ann, Lotta was hustled directly to performances and home again. Although she was approaching sixteen, there were still no boyfriends. Mary Ann made a habit of intervening and heading off any romance that might come Lotta's way. A supporting player in one of the stage plays Lotta performed in said she was "guarded like an odalisque in a harem." Most people referred to the cheerful Lotta as "Miss Lotta, the Unapproachable." Once, toward evening in the summer, a young man with a horse and carriage called to take her riding. Mary Ann sent him away quickly, but for days afterward, following dinner, Lotta contrived to sweep the front porch in case he should return. Unhappily, he did not.[23]

Lotta Crabtree was a true pin-up girl, even in her teens. She was the most fully pictured actress of her time, and her diversified moods always displayed themselves in her pictures. They were as much a part of herself and her acting as the flaming hair and coal-black eyes. Her dancing was as light as gossamer, when she wanted it to be, or boldly primitive. She was an excellent mimic, both in song and dance. She knew how to play the banjo, and she had a beautiful, flexible soprano voice with incredible range.

Lotta Crabtree was a popular star and in constant demand. By 1863 she was earning more than forty-two thousand dollars a year. Mary Ann was a smart businesswoman and invested her daughter's money in real estate. She walked the streets of the towns Lotta performed and bought vacant lots she believed would be highly sought after as the town grew. Lotta had no head for finances and counted on her mother to pay all her bills and support her act.[24]

At the peak of Lotta's fame in California, Lotta, her mother, and her brothers, George and John, traveled east. Lotta captured the hearts of theatergoers in New York, Chicago, Boston, and the Midwest. She performed in *Uncle Tom's Cabin* and *Jenny Leatherlungs*. One of her most popular plays was an adaptation of Dickens's The *Old Curiosity Shop* in which Lotta played two different characters. Lotta was fond of portraying young men. She had such a youthful face that she could get away with playing those kinds of roles, but Mary Ann objected. Not only did she think her child should be portraying queens and damsels in distress, but Lotta had an unladylike habit of plunging her hands into the pants of her costumes. Mary Ann sewed the pockets shut on her entire wardrobe.[25]

Her mother's overbearing actions never dampened Lotta's spirit. Lotta was thrilled with the praise she received from the audiences on the East Coast. In a letter to a friend in 1865 she wrote how she felt about the reception she was getting everywhere she performed:

I'm a continual success wherever I go. In some places I created quite a theatrical furor as they call it. I performed in Buffalo in a play called "Fanchon." The people were delighted and the theatre not big enough to hold them. . . . Why, friend Billie, your heart would jump for joy to see the respect I am treated with here among the theatre people. I'm a star and that is sufficient, and making quite a name.[26]

Even in her thirties Lotta always gave the impression of a young girl, never a woman, but a girl who delighted in flouting convention. She wore her skirts shorter than most, smoked thinly rolled black cigars, and sprinkled her hair with cayenne pepper to catch the reflection of the footlights.

Lotta's brothers, specifically Jack Crabtree, took the place of the men Lotta could have loved if her mother would have allowed her to have a romantic life. Jack was a forerunner of the Broadway playboys. His guests at lavish dinner parties ranged from Sarah Bernhardt, the greatest actress of her time (outside of Lotta, in Jack's opinion) to John Sullivan, heavyweight boxing champion of the world. He entertained all of the celebrities with Lotta playing on the bill.[27]

There were times when well-meaning friends scolded her for pampering her brother. Lotta's stock answer was: "Jack is all I live for. If I can't humor myself in this one way then I may as well stop living, too. I have no wants of my own."[28]

But she was secretly doing other things. While she and her mother were accumulating tremendously valuable real estate in Manhattan, Lotta was carrying on her own philanthropies, helping the less fortunate without publicity or fanfare.[29]

By 1870, Lotta was earning more than eighty thousand dollars a year and was one of the most popular actresses on the American stage. She spent a great deal of the allowance her mother gave her on her family, lavishing them with gold watches and fine clothes and sending her brothers to the best schools in the country. Mary Ann kept track of every dime Lotta spent and was convinced that if she didn't keep a close eye on her, the very generous Lotta would give away all the money she had. She was so protective of Lotta and her fortune she would fight anyone to keep them both intact. Mary Ann once caught her husband stealing coins from the steamer trunk where she stored Lotta's earnings. She was so outraged by his behavior that she had him arrested. Mary Ann felt John's actions would have a negative effect on Lotta's career and agreed not to press charges if he would leave the country. John reluctantly agreed. When Lotta and the rest of her family went abroad they met up with John in London.[30]

While touring Europe Lotta learned to paint, studied French, and took piano lessons. She drew attention everywhere she went. She would drive a pony cart up and down the streets dressed in white muslin and blue ribbons.[31]

When she returned to America in 1875, Lotta continued portraying children and playing younger parts in comical performances. She loved making people laugh and is considered by most historians as one of the theater's first comediennes. Lotta loved animals, and, when she finally returned to her beloved San Francisco to perform in yet another play, she purchased a fountain at the intersection of Kearney and Market Streets and donated it to the city so thirsty horses would have a place to get a drink.

Lotta retired from the theater in 1891. A fall on stage in Buffalo, New York, prompted her decision to leave the acting profession at the age of forty-five. All of her energy was diverted to the administration of the charities she had established. She and her mother retreated to a summer cottage on Lake Hopatcong, New Jersey, that she named Attol Tryst (Attol is Lotta spelled backward). It was a gift from mother to daughter but built with Lotta's money. It was one of the most elaborate homes in the area.[32]

Mary Ann Crabtree died in 1905. Lotta was beside herself with grief. Her constant companion and best friend was no longer at her side. Mary Ann didn't leave a will, but Lotta found more than seventy thousand dollars in cash hidden throughout their home. Twenty thousand of that was hidden inside a granite coffeepot. Lotta also found financial statements that showed the amount of money she had earned off the investments her mother had made for her. Mary Ann's investments had brought in more than two million dollars.[33]

Lotta sold the mansion on Lake Hopatcong and purchased the Brewster Home in Boston, where she lived a quiet, almost reclusive life. The remaining years of her life were spent painting and giving her money away. On many days she could be found on the streets of Boston fitting straw hats for horses to shade them from the heat.[34]

Lotta Crabtree died of arteriosclerosis in 1924 at the age of seventy-seven. She left her sizable estate to veterans, animals, students of music and agriculture, needy children at Christmas time, and needy actors. She was buried next to her mother in Woodlawn Cemetery in New York City. Regardless of the men who hoped to persuade Lotta to fall in love with them and spend the rest of her life in their company, she never married.[35]

Love Lessons Learned
by Maria Josefa Jaramillo

Let the man you love feel free to travel, especially after you get married. Kit Carson was a busy explorer. After three months of marriage, he joined an expedition across the unsettled frontier, leaving his new bride at home alone.

Be emotionally and spiritually grounded. Maria Josefa was devoted to the church and wanted the same in a husband. Kit appreciated that about Maria Josefa and her faithful example led to his conversion.

Show confidence. Be sure of yourself, and, like an explorer of the Old West, be ready to tackle whatever obstacle lies ahead of you. Maria Josefa withstood many hardships to run the home Kit built for her on the Little Cimarron River. He knew she could handle the job in his absence.

Appreciate a man's strengths. Maria Josefa knew her husband would never have been happy as a rancher. She encouraged him to do what he believed he was called to do, explore the rugged West.

Convey unconditional love. The strong relationship Maria Josefa and Kit enjoyed was based on the mutual respect they had for each other.

MARIA JOSEFA JARAMILLO

Love and the Explorer

On February 3, 1843, well-known and well-respected frontiersman and scout Christopher Houston Carson (better known as Kit Carson) escorted his bride, Maria Josefa Jaramillo, from Our Lady of Guadalupe Church in Taos, where they were married, to their new home not far away. Maria was Carson's third wife. He was thirty-three years old and she was fifteen. The couple was introduced by Carson's friend and an occasional employer, Charles Bent. Bent was a fur trader and explorer and was, coincidentally, married to Maria Josefa's sister, Ignacia.[1]

According to the May 16, 1907, edition of the Rio Rancho, New Mexico, newspaper, the *Rio Rancho Observer*, Carson was described as "short, balding and bowlegged." He saw in Maria Josefa "grace and elegance," and Maria Josefa saw in Carson "fearlessness and a sense of decency." Carson's friends agreed with Maria's assessment of his personality. History records that he wasn't afraid of "hell or high water" and that his private life was "as clean as a hound's tooth."[2]

Maria Josefa was born on March 19, 1828, in Santa Fe, New Mexico. Her father, Francisco Jaramillo, was a merchant, and her mother, Maria Apolonia Vigil, owned substantial acreage in the Rio Grande area of the state. Maria Josefa helped her parents maintain their ranch and cared for her younger brothers and sisters. She met Carson in Taos in 1842. He had been on an expedition with Colonel John Charles Frémont in the Rocky Mountains and was anxious to visit a place where there were

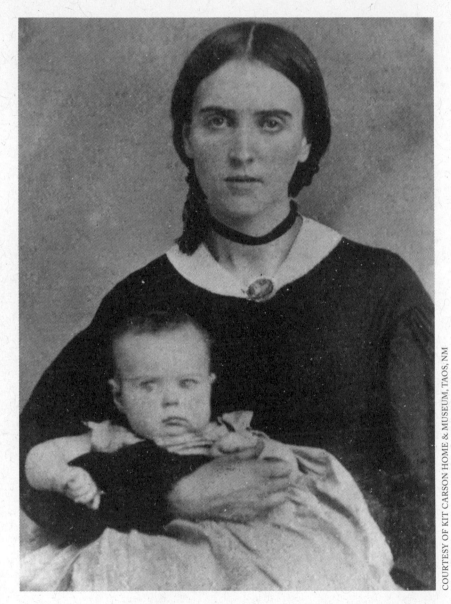

Maria Josefa Jaramillo was fifteen when she married Kit Carson. The pair was married more than twenty years.

lots of people. Historical records on hand at the Kit Carson Museum in Taos, New Mexico, note that Carson thought Maria Josefa was a lovely young woman.[3] Author and politician Gerrard Lewis noted that "her style of beauty was of the haughty, heart-breaking kind—such as would lead a man with a glance of the eye to risk his life for one smile."[4]

Although Maria Josefa and Carson were equally impressed with one another, her father would not permit them to marry because Carson was illiterate. Francisco was an educated man and very well respected in the community. He was aware of Carson's work as an accomplished scout, crisscrossing the western territories, but preferred his daughter marry someone with a scholastic background, at the very least someone who was a member of the Catholic faith. Carson was determined to make Maria Josefa his wife and decided to convert to Catholicism. He attended the necessary classes, counseled with a priest, and paid the fee required for a wedding ceremony in the church.[5]

According to the records on hand at the Catholic parish in Taos, "Cristobal Carson, thirty-two years old and a native of Missouri, the son of Linsey Carson and Rebecca Roberson, was baptized on January 28, 1843." Luise Lee and Maria Cruz Padilla are listed as his godparents. Padre Antonio Jose Martinez presided over the service. Carson and Maria Josefa were married nine days later on February 6, 1843. Her sister, Maria Ignacia, and her husband stood on either side of the couple when they exchanged vows.[6]

A short three months after the wedding, Carson left on the first of many expeditions he would participate in during his married life. Carson had been leading treks to various parts of the unsettled frontier since he was fifteen years old. He was born in Madison County, Kentucky, on December 24, 1809. Just after his first birthday his parents moved to Howard County, Missouri. Carson had five brothers and six sisters. His father was a lumberjack and died in a work-related accident

COURTESY LIBRARY OF CONGRESS, LC-USZ62-107570

Kit Carson's feats as a guide, scout, and Indian fighter were comparable to those of famous mountain man Daniel Boone.

when Carson was nine years old. At the age of fourteen he was an apprentice to a saddle maker, a job that he said "soon became irksome to him." He ran away (a one cent reward was offered for his return) and arrived in Santa Fe in the fall of 1826.[7]

The *Rio Rancho Observer* notes that the independent Carson had a talent for learning different languages. He mastered Spanish quickly and was able to communicate easily with people in New Mexico and other territories where he traveled. He spoke French and fifteen different Indian dialects, and knew sign language. Because he also had a talent with weapons, he was able to handle any trouble that came his way. He shot Native Americans who tried to interfere with his work as a hunter and trapper.[8]

In 1829 Carson hired on as an interpreter and accompanied copper mine owners to their property in Mexico. From there he joined a party of trappers traveling north to California over uncharted wilderness. He collected furs, hides, and elk, deer, and antelope meat to sell and trade at outposts along the Salt River and in the Rocky Mountains. While bravely blazing a westward trail for pioneers to follow later, Carson suffered lack of water, rugged terrain, and inhospitable weather. His daring reputation was proven in 1833 when he and fifty trappers were hunting along the Arkansas River in Colorado and a band of Crow Indians stole their horses. Carson led a dozen men forty miles through the snow to catch the thieves and retrieve their rides.[9]

Two years later Carson battled with the Blackfoot Indians in Wyoming. Employed by the Rocky Mountain Fur Company to supply military forts with food, Carson was leading more than one hundred trappers along the Green River when they were fired upon by Blackfoot Indians angry that smallpox had killed many in their tribe. With little ammunition Carson and the others managed to drive the Blackfoot Indians back to their encampment.[10]

Maria Josefa was not Carson's first venture into married life. An Arapaho woman named Waa-Nibe married him in the summer of 1835. Carson wasn't the only one vying for her affections. Another trapper wanted to marry her. In his autobiography, Carson recalled the fight he and the trapper had that earned him Waa-Nibe's hand:

There was in the party of Captain Drips a large Frenchman, one of those overbearing kind and very strong. He made a practice of whipping every man that he was displeased with and that was nearly all. One day, after he had beaten two or three men, he said that for Frenchmen he had no trouble to flog, and as for the Americans, he would take a switch and switch them. I did not like such talk from any man, so I told him that I was the worst American in the camp. Many could trash him, but they didn't on account of being afraid. I told him if he made use of anymore such expression I would rip his guts.[11]

He said nothing but started for his rifle, mounted his horse, and made his appearance in front of the camp. As soon as I saw him, I mounted my horse and took the first arms I could get ahold of, which was a pistol, galloped up to him and demanded if I was the one which he intended to shoot. Our horses were touching. He said no, but at the same time drawing his gun. We both fired at the same time; all present said but one report was heard. I shot him through the arm and his ball passed my head, cutting my hair and the powder burning my eye, the muzzle of his gun being near my head when he fired. During our stay in camp we had no more bother with this bully Frenchman.[12]

Carson and Waa-Nibe married shortly after the altercation with the French trapper. Historians and ancestors of both Carson and Maria Josefa admit that Waa-Nibe was the "true love of his life." Waa-Nibe died from a fever three years after the two were wed. The couple had two daughters. The youngest of the girls died in a tragic accident. Adaline, their oldest daughter, was entrusted to the care of one of Carson's sisters living in Missouri. Carson had joined an expedition traveling to Yellowstone and Bighorn and could not take the child with him.[13]

Once again Carson encountered problems with Native Americans living on the land. The Blackfoot Indians were so desperate to get rid of

Carson and the other mountain men with him that they set fire to the dry grass and brush around their camp. Carson managed to escape the blaze and continue on with the venture.

Between 1826 and 1842, Carson was a part of more than a dozen organized treks across the western wilderness. His reputation as a great frontiersman grew with each undertaking; from the Columbia River to the Rio Grande, through the Sierra and the Rocky Mountains, his powers of endurance were impressive to all who heard about them. According to the September 22, 1905, edition of the *Boston Globe*, Carson could go for days without food and did not tire easily. He always kept moving toward his destination, whether across the arid deserts of Arizona or the snowy cliffs of the Northern Sierras; he refused to be diverted from his route.[14]

In 1841, two years after he lost his first wife, Carson married a seventeen-year-old Cheyenne Indian woman named Making-Our-Road. The two became acquainted during a trip to Bent's Fort in Colorado. Carson had been contracted by the commander of the post to do some hunting for the troops. The extended time he spent away from his new bride working contributed to the demise of their union. Less than a year after they were married, Making-Our-Road decided she no longer wanted to be tied to Carson. When he returned to the Cheyenne tribe camp to see his wife, he found his personal belongings outside her lodge. According to Cheyenne custom that was her way of telling him she wanted him to be gone. She later migrated out of the area with other members of her tribe. A year after his marriage to Making-Our-Road ended, Carson met Maria Josefa.[15]

The survey trip Carson made with John Frémont before he wed Maria Josefa made him famous. As an employee with the US Corps of Topographical Engineers, Frémont was charged with mapping the country of the Platte River to the Rockies. Carson was paid one hundred dollars a month to serve as Frémont's guide, more than three times the amount he made as a hunter for military posts.[16]

Carson's true-life adventures working for Frémont and the military were translated into popular dime novels. Stories of how he led exploration teams across the plains, hunted buffalo, and tracked down Native Americans who attacked wagon trains, killed pioneers, and kidnapped women were read by thousands of emigrants traveling west. According to Carson's autobiography, his name and notoriety did not impress Francisco Jaramillo. Jaramillo had envisioned his daughter Maria Josefa marrying a much younger man. Carson's dedication to his Catholic conversion eventually won Maria Josefa's father's approval. "The custom was for the groom-to-be to furnish the bride with a complete trousseau," Carson noted in his memoirs. "The wedding feast took place in the home of the bride, but the bride groom's family [he was referring to Charles Bent and his wife, Ignacia] was completely in charge, and furnished everything for the occasion."[17]

Josefa spent much of her first year of marriage without her husband. Thirteen months passed between the time Carson left Taos in late May 1843 (shortly after they wed he joined Frémont as a guide and scout on another excursion) and his return. Josefa maintained the cabin Carson built for her on the Little Cimarron River, alone. Carson spent the time apart from his wife (whom he called "Chipeta," which means "little singing bird") leading still more expeditions across the western territories, clearing crude paths for future travelers while others on the journey recorded astronomical and topographical findings. He kept the company he was hired to work for safe from warring Native Americans and wild animals.[18]

When war broke out between the United States and Mexico, Carson joined in the fight and served daringly. His actions on the field of battle earned him a personal appointment from President James K. Polk as lieutenant of rifles.[19]

Between the end of the Mexican War and start of the Civil War, Carson and his friend Lucien Maxwell began a ranching and farming operation on Maxwell's property in Rayado, New Mexico, fifty miles away from Taos. Josefa was finally able to spend a great deal of time with her husband as he tried to adapt to the life of a gentleman rancher. No matter how Carson tried to rid himself of the desire of traipsing into uncharted territory, he couldn't. Josefa recognized that Carson was not meant to lead a life working the land. She could see he was much more interested in protecting her, their family, friends, and his business associates from frequent raids by the Indians in the southern plains and the desert. Many Apache, Ute, Comanche, and Cheyenne Indians around Carson's ranch stole horses, livestock, and personal possessions from those trying to settle in the Rayodo area and those living in Taos. Before Carson could get his wife out of the volatile situation, Josefa gave birth to their first child. Charles Bent Carson was born one month premature in May 1849. The baby was too frail to make a grueling journey. Carson and his family decided to stay behind with the Maxwells and a few others who had come to the settlement hoping to find gold in the nearby Sangre de Cristo Mountains.[20]

In October, Carson was called upon by the military to help locate several pioneers who had been separated from wagon trains traveling to the Cimarron Cutoff. It didn't take Carson long to find the men in the party. All had been killed by Apache Indians and their bodies were strewn along the trail. The women and children with the train had been taken hostage. Carson tracked the women to an abandoned Indian camp and discovered they had been killed. The children were never found. Carson returned to Taos to be with his wife and their infant son. The baby's health had never fully improved from his early birth, and he died in 1851.[21]

Carson and Josefa had a second son in October 1852 and named him William. Four months after the baby was born, Carson decided to help drive sheep to California. He had heard that pioneers were willing to pay large sums of money for the animals. Carson and a friend rounded up sixty-five hundred head of sheep and along with twenty-two hands pushed them west. His arrival into Nevada with the animals attracted the attention of newspapers in Northern California. It drew a barrage of unwelcome attention to him. Carson was pointed out wherever he went. He was given free passes on steamboats and all places of amusement and was harassed by people while he tried to eat.[22]

Once he sold his sheep (at $5.50 a head), he hurried home to Josefa and William, vowing to make more of an attempt to be content with a quiet life on the ranch.[23] The Carsons had now been married nine years, and he had spent more than half of that time away from Josefa. Just as he was adapting to being a full-time husband and father, the US government appointed him Indian agent for the Ute, Apache, and Pueblo Indians. Carson was devoted to serving the Native Americans he represented well, and Josefa supported him in his efforts. There were times when the couple used their own earnings to help feed the Indians who were not getting the provisions promised to them by Washington politicians.[24] According to a report issued by Carson to the Bureau of Indian Affairs in 1859, "Scarcely a day passes but I have five to twenty-five to feed and take care of—their only resource is upon the government."[25]

Carson and Josefa adopted three Indian orphans during his tenure as an Indian agent. The pair also had two more children of their own in that time: a daughter, born in 1856, and a son born in 1858.[26]

When the Civil War broke out in April 1861, Carson resigned his post with the Bureau of Indian Affairs and joined the Union Army. He was made lieutenant colonel of the New Mexico volunteers and was required to meet in Albuquerque with the other soldiers from the territory in June 1861. Josefa and family went with him. On August 2, Josefa gave birth to another boy. The Carsons named him after their son who had died. Carson was not shy about showing his love for his wife and children. An officer in the New Mexico volunteers, Captain Rafael Chacon, wrote in his memoirs about the touching scene he witnessed between the mountain man and his brood. "He used to lie down on an Indian blanket, in front of his quarters, with his pockets full of candy and lumps of sugar," Chacon recalled. "His children would jump on top of him and take the candy and sugar from his pockets and eat it . . . and he derived great pleasure from these little episodes. He was most kind to his wife, Dona Josefa Jaramillo."[27]

Carson distinguished himself during the Civil War at the Battle of Valverde. He led his troops across the Valverde River to engage more than four hundred Confederate troops in combat. Heavy cannon fire from rebel cannons eventually pushed Carson and his troops back across the river and onto Fort Craig in Socorra County, New Mexico. Fort commander Colonel E. R. S. Canby left the post to lead soldiers to a skirmish with the Confederates at Glorieta Pass.[28] In his absence he put Carson in charge and gave orders to defend the camp from any attack. When Carson learned that the Confederates were not going to advance on the fort but bypass it instead and press on in the direction of Taos, he sent word to Josefa to leave the area.[29]

Josefa wasted no time gathering her family together. She quickly ushered them out of town and to safety. Fearing the advancing troops might overtake Taos and raid the Carson home looking for valuables, Josefa decided to take the money and jewels she had tucked away with her when they departed. She hid the items on an Indian girl she and Carson were raising. During their mad dash from Taos, the Carson family met a band of Ute Indians with a three-year-old Navajo boy in tow. The Utes complained to Josefa that the toddler was a bother and that they were going to kill him. She could not bear the idea of the boy's life being taken and decided to bargain for him. After trading one of the horses she had with her for the child, Josefa hurried off with her family. When Carson and Josefa were reunited she told him what had transpired. The couple adopted the boy and named him Juan Carson.[30]

Carson resigned from military service in 1865, but any hope Josefa had that he would return home to stay was dashed when her husband accepted the position of superintendent of Indian Affairs for the Colorado Territory. In 1866 he moved his family to Boggsville, Colorado, where he briefly took command of daily operation at Fort Garland in the southern portion of the territory. Not long after they arrived at the post, Josefa gave birth to their third daughter.[31]

By July 1867, Carson's health was rapidly deteriorating. An accident he had suffered some months before taking the job as superintendent of Indian Affairs for the Colorado Territory was causing him problems. During one of his many trips across the West, a rattlesnake had spooked his horse. Carson was hurled over an embankment and injured his neck. At the age of fifty-seven, riding a horse was excruciatingly painful for him. He traveled primarily by army ambulance. Carson used an army ambulance to transport himself and a delegation of Ute chiefs to Washington, DC, in February 1868. They made it as far as Fort Lyon (more than 147 miles from their starting point) using the ambulance. The remainder of the trip was made via stagecoach and railroad. The purpose Carson had for enduring such hardship was to negotiate a treaty concerning tribal lands.[32]

When it came time to return to Colorado in March 1868, Carson was weak and exhausted. Josefa was expecting their seventh child, and he wanted nothing more than to be with her. "My wife must see me," he reportedly told the Ute chiefs who made the journey east with him.

"If I was to write about this, [referring to how ill he truly was] or died out here, it would kill her. I must get home . . ."[33]

On April 11, 1868, Josefa met Carson at La Juanita, Colorado, with a team and a wagon to take him home. The Carsons welcomed their seventh child into the world on April 13, 1868. Two weeks after their daughter was born, Josefa died of complications from that birth. Carson was heartbroken over the loss of his wife and overwhelmed by the prospect of caring for his large family alone. The financial burden worried him as well.[34] The income earned as military man, superintendent, and former trapper was meager. "I fear I have not done right by my children," Carson confided in his friend William T. Sherman, concerning the little wealth he had to pass on.[35]

A month after Josefa's death Carson passed away. He died of a ruptured abdominal aneurism on May 23, 1868, at Fort Lyon, Colorado. The June 4, 1868, edition of the Decatur, Illinois, newspaper, *The Decatur Review*, reported on the frontiersman's accomplishments, "No one man did more than Kit Carson in expediting the development of the wilderness of the Great West." Carson and Josefa were buried at the cemetery in Boggsville, Colorado. Their bodies were later moved to a cemetery in Taos, New Mexico.[36]

Love Lessons Learned
by Luzena Stanley Wilson

Know that the best way to a gold miner's heart and fortune and is through his stomach.

❦

Be ready to capitalize on your strengths. Luzena earned a living as well as her husband's adoration using her skills as a cook, boardinghouse owner-operator, and a banker.

❦

Be willing to rebuild, no matter the disaster. Luzena didn't spend time feeling sorry for her losses when all was destroyed in a fire and a flood; she believed in the power of resurrection and rebuilt.

❦

Remember that some men (in the Old West) eventually tire of a strong, successful woman. Those ladies knew what they wanted and were not fragile.

❦

Take time from work and business ventures to know when your husband is thinking of leaving . . . and never coming back.

LUZENA STANLEY WILSON

Love and the Gold Miner

Luzena Stanley Wilson stood in the center of her empty, one-room log home in Andrew County, Missouri, studying the opened trunk in front of her. All of her worldly possessions were tucked inside it: family Bibles, two quilts, one dress, a bonnet, a pair of shoes, and a few pieces of china. Mason Wilson, Luzena's husband of five years, marched into the house just as she closed the lid on the trunk and fastened it tightly. They exchanged a smile, and Mason picked up the trunk and carried it outside. Luzena took a deep breath and followed after him. In a few short moments they were off on a journey west to California. It was May 1, 1849, Luzena's birthday. She was thirty years old.[1]

The Wilsons were farmers with two sons: Thomas, born in September 1845, and Jay, born in June 1848. Three payments had been made on the plot of land the Wilsons purchased in January 1847. Prior to news of the Gold Rush captivating Mason's imagination, the plan was to work the multi-acre homestead and pass the farm on to their children and their children's children.[2]

Rumors that the mother lode awaited anyone who dared venture into California's Sierra foothills prompted Mason to abandon the farm and travel to the rugged mountains beyond Sacramento. In addition to Luzena and her husband, their sons, her brothers, and their wives had committed to travel to California as well. A train of five wagons was organized to transport the sojourners west. On the off

Nevada City in 185

COURTESY SEARLS HISTORICAL LIBRARY

Nevada City, California, where Luzena Stanley Wilson opened one of the area's first hotels, as it looked in 1852

chance Mason never found a fortune in gold, the couple left behind funds with the justice of the peace to make another payment on their homestead. In the event the Wilsons were able to stake out a claim for themselves in the Gold Country, they would sell their Missouri home and use the proceeds to aid in their new life.[3]

"It was the work of but a few days to collect our forces for the march," Luzena recorded in her journal shortly after they left on the first leg of their trip. "We never gave a thought to selling our section [of land], but left it. I little realized then the task I had undertaken. If I had, I think I should have stayed in Andrew County." It would take five months for the Wilsons to reach their westward destination. Most of the belongings Luzena packed in their prairie schooner would be lost or left behind on the trail because they proved to be too burdensome to continue hauling.[4]

Luzena described the long journey west in her memiors as "plodding, unvarying monotony, vexations, exhaustions, throbs of hope and depth of despair." Dusty, short-tempered, always tired, and with their patience as tattered as their clothing, the Wilson family and thousands like them plodded on and on. They were scorched by heat; enveloped in dust that reddened their eyes and parched their throats; and were bruised, scratched, and bitten by innumerable insects.[5]

Luzena's Quaker upbringing in North Carolina had not prepared her for such a grueling endeavor. Her parents, Asa and Diane Hunt, had relocated from Piedmont, North Carolina, to Saint Louis in 1843, but the trip was comparatively easy. After the Hunts arrived in Missouri, they purchased a number of acres of land at a government auction. Luzena lived on the family farm until she and Mason wed on December 19, 1844.[6]

The first day of the Wilsons' journey to California was without incident. It wasn't until the sun began to sink slowly in the sky and Mason announced it was time to make camp that Luzena became terrified. "Our first campfire was lighted in Indian Territory, which spread in one unbroken, unnamed waste from the Missouri River to the border line of California," she shared in her journal. "Around us in every direction were groups of Indians sitting, standing, and on horseback, as many as two hundred in the camp. I had read and heard whole volumes of their bloody deeds, the massacre of harmless white men, torturing helpless women, carrying away captive children the most precious in the wide world, and I lived in an agony of dread that first night."[7]

Luzena noted in her memoirs that the Indians never posed any threat to her or her family. She admitted they were in more danger from the elements and terrain than any Native Americans they encountered along the way. Torrential downpours, swollen rivers, prairie fires, and knee-high snowdrifts impeded their progress and at times exhausted their resources. Luzena wrote in her journal:

The winter rains and melting snow saturated the earth like a sponge, and the wagons sunk like lead in the sticky mud. Sometimes a whole day was consumed in going two or three miles, and one day we made camp but a quarter of a mile distance from the last. The last days were spent in digging out both animals and wagon, and the light of the campfire was utilized to mend broken bolts and braces. We built the fire at night close to the wagon, under which we slept. To add to the miseries of the trip it rained, and one night when the wagon was mired and we could not shelter under it, we slept with our feet pushed under it and an old cotton umbrella spread over our faces. Sometimes we went down the mountains, they were so steep we tied great trees behind to keep the wagon from falling over the oxen; and once when the whole surface of the mountain side was smooth, slippery rock, the oxen stiffened their legs, and the wagon and all literally slid down a quarter of a mile. But the longest way has an end. At last we caught a glimpse of the miners' huts far down in the gulch and reached the end of our journey.[8]

In spite of the overwhelming challenges the Wilsons faced en route to California, many travelers before them considered them to be fortunate. Gravel markers lined the wagon trail west. Burials were common, especially when cholera struck. Some died in battles fought with Native Americans trying to protect their lands, but more succumbed to illness, accidents, and to violence among wagon train members. Women died during childbirth along the way, and their children fell before all manner of diseases and fatal mishaps.

Luzena, Mason, and their children were among the more than twenty-five thousand people who came west in 1849. The journal she started at the beginning of their harrowing trip did not end when she arrived in California on October 1, 1849. Luzena wrote about her time at the immigrant campsite in Sacramento where the family initially settled. "The population was about two thousand wood buildings, forty-five cloth and tent, three hundred campfires, etc., in the open air and under trees," Luzena recorded in her memoirs about the Gold Rush town.[9]

Given the daily growth of the area, Luzena determined there was a great need for a boardinghouse. Mason agreed, and the two decided to go into the hospitality business. They sold their oxen for six hundred dollars and purchased a hotel called the Trumbow House. The majority of boarders at the Trumbow House were men. There were few women in Sacramento or the outlying gold mining camps. Luzena's homemaking skills were well received and in high demand. Guests were charged $17.50 a week for a clean room, laundry services, and savory meals. During the two months she operated the boardinghouse there was never a vacant room. Every day more and more immigrants poured in from the plains or got off the steamers that brought them to California via the Isthmus of Panama— each one was eager to get to the mountains to hunt for gold. "The world will never see the like again of those 'pioneers of 49,'" Luzena recalled in her journal. "They were, as a rule, uptight, energetic, and hard-working, many of them men of education and culture whom the misfortune of poverty had forced into the ranks of labor in this strange country."[10]

A major flood in Sacramento, combined with a flurry of excitement about gold nuggets lying in the streets of Nevada City, prompted Mason to uproot his family again and head for the hills in March

1850. Nevada City was sixty miles from Sacramento. The Wilsons lacked the funds to purchase a wagon and team to get to the boomtown. A miner with a vehicle and horse was on his way to Nevada City and offered to take Luzena, Mason, her boys, a stove, and two sacks of flour with him for seven hundred dollars. "This looked hopeless, and I told him I guessed we wouldn't go as we had no money," she explained in her memoirs. "I must have carried my honesty in my face, for he looked at me a minute and said, 'I'll take you, Ma'am, if you will assure me the money.' I promised him it should be paid, if I lived, and we made the money. So, pledged to a new master, Debt, we pressed forward on the road. It took twelve days to make it to the bustling mining camp. A row of canvas tents lined each of the two ravines leading to the tent city, and the gulches were crawling with men panning for gold. Donner Pass, a seven-thousand-foot barricade of naked rock lay, beyond the camp.[11]

Mason was in a hurry to start his search for gold. After he built a crude shelter to help keep his wife and children warm and dry, he hurried off to stake out a claim. Luzena quickly went to work unpacking, making beds, and firing up her stove. As she worked she contemplated how she was going to help make good on the cost it took to transport her family to the area. "As always occurs to the mind of a woman, I thought of taking in boarders," she wrote in her journal. "So I bought two boards from a precious pile belonging to a man who was building the second wooden house in town. [This was the start of the Wilson Hotel in Nevada City.] With my own hands I chopped stakes, drove them into the ground, and set up my table. I bought provisions from a neighboring store, and when my husband came back at night he found, mid the weird light of the pine torches, twenty miners eating at my table. Each man as he rose put a $1 in my hand and said I might count him as a permanent customer."[12]

Within six weeks of opening her business, Luzena had earned enough to pay the money owed to the miner who brought the Wilsons to Nevada. She also expanded and renovated the hotel and purchased a new stove. By the end of the summer in 1850, Luzena had an average of seventy-five to two hundred boarders living at the establishment, each paying twenty-five dollars a week.[13]

She named her establishment El Dorado after the fabled kingdom in Spanish America supposedly rich in precious metals and jewels, which had lured sixteenth-century explorers away from their homes. In addition to the clean accommodations offered at Luzena's were her biscuits. It was not uncommon for men who survived on a regular diet of beans and bacon to offer Luzena five dollars for one biscuit. The hotel's reputation grew, attracting more and more customers. Late in 1850, Luzena expanded her commercial enterprise, hiring cooks and waiters.[14]

It was clear to Luzena that the best way to strike it rich in a gold camp was to provide the necessities of life to the miners swinging pick axes and dumping dirt into rockers and gold pans. Mason agreed and abandoned his quest for a strike. Luzena then made him her business partner. The couple expanded their holdings. They built a mercantile and furnished it with all the supplies prospectors needed.

After six months of hard work, Luzena's El Dorado Hotel was estimated to be worth ten thousand dollars, and the stock of goods in the new store was worth even more. "The buildings were of the roughest possible description," Luzena noted in her journal. "They were to Nevada City what the Palace Hotel was to San Francisco."[15]

Not long after the Wilson's mercantile opened for business, Luzena recognized a need for a bank in the area and determined to provide for the growing community. "There was no place of deposit for money," Luzena noted in her memoirs, "and the men living in the house dropped into the habit of leaving their [gold] dust with me for safe keeping. At times I have had a larger amount of money in my charge than would furnish capital for a country bank." Luzena did provide capital for Nevada City residents at 10 percent interest on loans. Her kitchen was also her bank vault. "Many a night have I shut my oven door on two milk-pans filled high with bags of gold dust," she wrote in her memoirs, "and I have often slept with my mattress literally lined with the precious metal. And at one time I must have had more than $200,000 lying unprotected in my bedroom . . ."[16]

Luzena never worried about being robbed. According to her journal entries, "lawbreakers were dealt with quickly and harshly." On July 22, 1850, she witnessed the severe punishment inflicted upon a man who had stolen a mule. "He did not travel far before he was overtaken and brought before a jury," the *Sacramento Transcript* newspaper reported on the scene. "He was found guilty of theft, not only of the mule, but also the earnings of the young man who had placed confidence in him, [and who] gave him his bag of gold dust to take out. . . . The verdict of guilty was given . . . and his punishment twenty-five lashes on his bare back, and [he was] compelled to work at $5 per day . . ."[17]

Luzena enjoyed eighteen months of prosperity before she, Mason, and her sons, along with eight thousand other Nevada City residents, were left homeless and practically destitute. "Some careless hand had set fire to a pile of pine shavings lying at the side of the house in course of construction," Luzena recorded in her memoirs, "and while we slept, unconscious of danger, the flames caught and spread, and in a short half hour the whole town was in a blaze." The Wilsons lost nearly everything they owned. Mason had five hundred dollars in his pocket he had forgotten to place in the stove the night before. The couple used that money to make a new start for themselves.[18]

Luzena found a few pieces of unburned canvas and some wooden planks; Mason pulled her stove from the ruins of the boardinghouse, and the pair set up another eatery. Once everything was in place, Luzena wasted no time returning to what she did best, which was cooking. Her culinary skills were popular during the rebuilding of the mining camp. She provided meals from dawn until dusk at prices she believed the struggling community could tolerate. In early July 1850, a prospector who appeared as though he could not afford anything gave Luzena a gold claim in exchange for one of her delicious dinners. The gold claim was a half a block from where her business had stood before the fire. He told her he had removed sixteen thousand dollars from the mine the day before. She eagerly agreed to the payment, imagining the mine would be a quick way to renew the fortune she had lost. Mason was opposed to the idea, however, and didn't want to work a claim. He felt the painstaking effort seldom resulted in a rich find and that the prospector had probably located all the gold to be had on that spot. Luzena sold the property for one hundred dollars to a miner. A few days prior to the Wilsons leaving the area to move back to Sacramento, the miner pulled ten thousand dollars in gold out of the diggings.[19]

Unlike the time it took for the Wilsons to travel to Nevada City, it was only a two-day journey returning to Sacramento. During their stay in Nevada City the roads had been drastically improved.

Luzena and Mason purchased another boardinghouse in Sacramento. "We took possession of a deserted hotel which stood on K Street," Luzena wrote in her memoirs. "This hotel was tenanted only by rats that galloped madly over the floor and made journeys from room to room through openings they had gnawed in the panels. . . . At the time, Sacramento was infested with the horrible creatures."[20]

After three months, the Wilsons moved on to a valley north of Sacramento called Benicia. The beautiful area was ideal for the pair and their children. Their goal was to purchase land and stay there for

Luzena Stanley Wilson, California Gold Rush entrepreneur,
1821–1902

the rest of their lives. "We were again penniless, however, and felt that we must get to work," Luzena noted in her journal. "Hay was selling in San Francisco at a $150 a ton, so my husband, leaving me to my own resources, set hard at work cutting and making hay; and I, as before, set up my stove and camp kettle and hung out my sign, printed with charred fire-brand on a piece of board, it read Wilson's Hotel."[21]

Within six months of opening, Luzena had earned a substantial amount of money, and the Wilson's Hotel had earned the reputation of being the best on the route from Sacramento to Benicia. Mason supplied the variety of meat Luzena served to her boarders. Elk, antelope, geese, pheasant, cattle, and bear were all on the menu at various times. On April 21, 1851, the Wilsons were able to purchase two hundred acres of land along Alamo Creek. Seven months later they bought three parcels in Vaca and another one hundred acres south of town.[22]

Mason's hay business was as profitable as Luzena's boardinghouse. For a time things were going very well for the pair and their sons, and then a heavy, substantial rain came and wiped out Mason's crops. Not long after that, government surveyors came to officially lay out the town of Benicia in Vaca Valley. They divided the valley including all the land the Wilsons had purchased. Immigrants quickly moved in and squatted on Luzena and Mason's property. "My husband was furious," Luzena recalled in her memoirs. "He swore that he would either have the land or kill every man who disputed his ownership. He left the house on an errand of ejectment, taking with him a witness, in case he should be killed or be forced to kill the squatters, many of whom knew and feared his reckless and determined purpose, would not have hesitated to dispose of him with a bullet."[23]

The courts were called upon to intercede and settle the matter; in the interim, the Wilsons moved from Benicia to Vaca Valley. Using the profits made from the Wilson's Hotel, Luzena bought lumber and bricks to build the family's home and a new boardinghouse business. The wooden structure was the first one of its kind built in Vaca Valley. Luzena's new business was as successful as her previous one. Well-respected judges, such as Murray Morrison and Justice Serranus

Clinton Hastings of the California Supreme Court, were frequent guests at the establishment.[24]

In January 1855, Luzena and Mason welcomed a third son to their family, Mason Jr. In May 1857, the couple welcomed a daughter, Correnah. The Wilsons continued to invest the money made from Luzena's boardinghouse in real estate. By the end of 1859, Luzena and Mason owned a considerable portion of the Vaca Valley town site and more than five hundred acres of surrounding lands.[25]

By 1858, the Wilsons had outgrown the small, temporary hotel they initially built in the area and decided to have a new one constructed at a cost of fourteen thousand dollars. The new business had two stories, a billiard room, and a large parlor. Mason became an agent for the Wells Fargo Company and operated the Wells Fargo office out of the hotel.[26]

In December 1872, after twenty-eight years of marriage, Mason abandoned his wife and family to travel to Missouri and Texas. Luzena never saw Mason again. Rumors circulated during that time suggested that Mason might have been suffering from a mental illness. Other people insisted that he had simply become miserable living with Luzena. Willis Jepson, one of Mason's friends, wrote a letter to the Wilsons' oldest son Jay explaining why he believed Mason chose to leave his home and family. "Luzena, Forty-Niner, was a determined and strong-minded personage—a woman of the real pioneer type," Jepson noted. "But even so her husband, your father, became wearied. He could stand Luzena no longer and went away from Vaca Valley. He put as much distance between himself and Luzena as well as he could." Ten years after Mason left Luzena and California, word came from an attorney in Waco, Texas, that he had passed away.[27]

In 1881, Luzena's daughter helped her compile her remembrances into a book entitled *Argonaut: A Woman's Reminiscences of Early Days.*

Solano County historian Sabine Goerke-Shrode called Luzena's book "an important historical source illustrating the Gold Rush from a woman's perspective."[28]

On July 11, 1902, Luzena died of thyroid cancer. She was eighty-three years old. According to her obituary, which ran in the July 12, 1902, edition of the *Woodland Daily Democrat* newspaper, Luzena's funeral service was held at her daughter's home. "Mrs. Wilson was a respected pioneer of Solano County, and was for many years a resident of Vaca Valley," the notice informed readers. "Mrs. Wilson was a noble woman and her death will be profoundly regretted."[29]

Love Lessons Learned
by Zoe Agnes Stratton

Dazzle him with your smarts and be unique. Friends and neighbors described Zoe as being "unlike any other woman Marshal Tilghman had ever met."

Appreciate his years of experience on the job and the job he wants to take on. Bill's first wife would have preferred that he not had gone into law enforcement. Zoe objected only to the danger to which he exposed himself and not the work itself.

Find inspiration in your partner. Zoe was an author of western books and in many respects Bill was her muse. Being his wife's inspiration endeared her to him.

Be willing to take on his family from a previous marriage. Zoe moved into the home Bill shared with his first wife and tried to make a life with his children, but they didn't receive it well. Still, she tried.

Accept that justice needed a firm hand in the Old West and that your husband was that hand.

ZOE AGNES STRATTON

Love and the Lawman

Lawman Bill Tilghman opened his eyes to flickering candlelight. He was in a bunk, covered with blankets. His shoulder was aching and stiff with bandages. He was thirstier than he could ever remember. He turned his head slowly and the movement brought a woman's figure out of the shadows. "How are you feeling?" said a quiet voice. "Thirsty," Bill mumbled. A tin cup of water was held to his lips. Bill drained it and sighed with satisfaction. In the thin candlelight Bill looked gaunt, his face hawkish, and his hair was grizzled to silver in spots. "You've lost a lot of blood," the woman said, sitting down beside him. "You need to stay put." Bill closed his eyes, and sleep took him.[1]

Golden sunlight was slanting through a window when Bill awoke. His head was clear, his eyes no longer fuzzy. He was hungry as a wolf. There beside him was his wife, Zoe, the woman he had seen by his side the night before. Bill was a US marshal in the Oklahoma territory. An encounter with a pair of desperate criminals who were trying to smuggle whiskey onto a Native American reservation in 1903 had left him seriously injured. Zoe had tended to his wounds and stayed with him until he was able to get back on his feet.[2]

The pair hadn't been married long, but Zoe knew her husband's job as a lawman was dangerous and was prepared to do all she could to support him. William Matthew Tilghman became a law enforcement officer in 1877. He was, according to his friend and one-time fellow

Bill Tilghman exemplified the idea of the lawman in the American Old West.

lawman Bat Masterson, "the best of all of us." Bat was referring to all the lawmen in the West. Zoe didn't disagree.[3]

Born on November 15, 1880, in Kansas, Zoe Agnes Stratton was twenty-three when she married Bill. He was more than twenty years older than she, but he suited the schoolteacher turned author perfectly. "He was a Christian gentleman," Zoe told reporters at the *Ada Evening News* on April 16, 1960. "He was quiet, kindly, greatly respected, and loved."[4]

Born on July 4, 1854, to an army soldier turned farmer and a young homemaker, Bill spent his early childhood in the heart of Sioux Indian territory in Minnesota. Grazed by an arrow when he was a baby, he was raised to respect Native Americans and protect his family from tribes that felt they had been unfairly treated by the government. Bill was one of six children. His mother insisted he had been "born to a life of danger."[5]

In 1859 his family moved to a homestead near Atkinson, Kansas. While Bill's father and oldest brother were off fighting in the Civil War, he worked the farm and hunted game. One of the most significant events in his life occurred when he was twelve years old while returning home from a blackberry hunt. His hero, Marshal Bill Hickok (Wild Bill), rode up beside him and asked if he had seen a man ride through with a team of mules and a wagon.[6]

The wagon and mules had been stolen in Abilene, and the marshal had pursued the culprit across four hundred miles. Bill told Hickok that the thief had passed him on the road that led to Atkinson. The marshal caught the criminal before he left the area and escorted him back to the scene of the crime. Bill was so taken by Hickok's passion for upholding the law he decided to follow in his footsteps and become a scout and lawman.[7]

Bill Tilghman set out on his own in 1871 and became a buffalo hunter. Using the Sharps rifle his father had given him, the eighteen-year-old learned the trade quickly and was an exceptional shot. He secured a contract with the railroad's owners to provide workers laying track to Fort Dodge, Kansas, and the subsequent town that grew close to it, Dodge City, with buffalo meat.

From September 1, 1871, to April 1, 1872, Bill killed and delivered three thousand buffalo. He set an all-time record, surpassing the previous one made by Wild Bill Hickok. Bill Tilghman's success as a buffalo hunter was due in part to his relationship with the Plains Indians. He never invaded their hunting grounds and treated them with dignity and reverence not commonly displayed by white men.[8]

Bill's extensive knowledge of the territory prompted cattle barons like Matt Childers to hire him to round up his livestock roaming about the area and then drive them to the market at Dodge. He was exceptional at the job, but his true ambition was to become a law enforcement officer. He was a natural at settling disputes between friends and competitors engaged in heated arguments, a necessity for any policeman. Army colonels and other high-ranking military leaders wanting to help settle differences between themselves and angry Native Americans sought out Bill. Although he would not wage war with the Indians against the United States, he did understand their bitter feeling toward the white men. In hopes of driving the Cheyenne, Crow, and Blackfoot out of the country, the government ordered that their main source of food be slaughtered. The mighty buffalo was hunted to near extinction.

With the buffalo gone, Bill was forced to find other employment. From 1873 to 1878, he worked as a merchant, contractor, land speculator, horse racer, cavalry scout, and livery stable and saloon owner. He ran the Crystal Palace with his business partner, Henry Garris.[9]

The Palace was located on the south side of Dodge City, and refinements to the tavern made the news on July 21, 1877. According to the *Dodge City Times*, "Garris and Tilghman's Crystal Palace is receiving a new front and an awning, which will tend to create a new attraction towards [*sic*] the never ceasing fountains of refreshments flowing within." Bill also owned and operated a ranch thirteen miles outside of Dodge, one that he would never relinquish.[10]

As a proprietor of the Crystal Palace, some of the customers he befriended had questionable, and sometimes criminal, backgrounds. It was guilt by association that led to his arrest on suspicion of being one of the notorious Kinsley train robbers. On February 9, 1878, the *Dodge City Times* reported that "William Tilghman, a citizen of Dodge City, was arrested on the same serious charge of attempt to rob the train. He stated that he was ready for trial, but the State asked for 10 days delay to procure witnesses, which was granted. Tilghman gave bail. It is generally believed that William Tilghman had no hand in the attempted robbery." The charges were dismissed four days after the arrest.[11]

Two months later, Bill was arrested for horse theft. A pair of stolen horses found at his livery implicated him in the crime. A thorough investigation proved that he had not been involved, as reported in the April 23, 1878, edition of the *Ford County Globe*.[12]

In the spring of 1877, he married Widow Flora Kendall and moved her and her baby to his Bluff Creek Ranch. Tilghman was now a respected family man and cattleman in Ford County. When Bat Masterson was elected sheriff of Dodge City in early 1878, one of his first orders of business was to hire Bill on as his deputy. In spite of Bill's encounters with the law, he was certain the esteemed Tilghman would be a positive addition to the force. Bat knew about Bill's reputation with a gun and his knowledge of Kansas and the surrounding territory. He also knew Bill didn't drink, which meant there'd never be a question of alcohol affecting his judgment. "I've seen many a man get killed just because his hand was a little unsteady or slow on the draw, when he had a few drinks in him," Bill maintained.[13]

Bill was dedicated to his position and approached his law enforcement duties, which included maintaining the office and records, feeding prisoners, and supervising the jail, with quiet determination. He wasn't content with solely keeping the peace; he wanted to know all about the legal process and proper methods of gathering evidence.

Unlike his mentor Bat Masterson and his idol Bill Hickok, who focused primarily on apprehending criminals using any means possible, Bill challenged himself to work within the confines of the law. Friend and foe alike appreciated his due diligence.[14]

In 1897, Flora Tilghman contracted tuberculosis and went to live with her mother in Dodge City. Her marriage to Bill had been strained for some years. Historical records indicate she didn't care for Bill being a lawman. She was left alone a great deal. She didn't like living in Oklahoma where Bill had taken a job as peace officer in the town of Perry. Flora filed for divorce shortly after returning to Kansas. She died three years later from tuberculosis. Flora and Bill had three children together, two girls and a boy. The oldest, Dorothy, was twenty when her mother passed away.[15]

Zoe and Bill met in 1900. Her father, Mayo Stratton, and Bill were friends. According to biographer Floyd Miller, "Zoe was not quite like any other girl he had ever known. She rode with the cowhands who worked her father's ranch, wrote poetry, and had attended college." Friends and neighbors described her as "a woman who could accomplish anything she set her mind to." Zoe and Bill began corresponding while she was away at school in Norman, Oklahoma, studying to be a teacher. He proposed to her while she was home visiting her family over Christmas vacation in 1902, and they were married on July 15, 1903.[16]

After a brief honeymoon in Kansas City, Zoe moved into the home Bill had shared with Flora. Bill's children resented their stepmother. Although she wisely did not try to come between them and their father, they never warmed to her. Dorothy especially felt the age difference between Zoe and her father was too great and believed this new woman in his life would eventually leave. The only thing that held them together was pride in Bill and the position he held in the county. According to Floyd Miller, "Bill was an influential man and was daily called up for advice on everything from family quarrels to business ethics."[17]

In addition to teaching school, Zoe was an aspiring author of westerns. Her life with Bill offered great insight into the stories she wrote. It was a rugged, lawless time with numerous renegades roaming the region. Zoe noted in her memoirs that Bill slept with a loaded .45 under his pillow to protect his wife, and eventually the three sons they had together, from fugitives he had once arrested seeking to gun him down. "He was adept at shooting with either hand, but generally carried one six-shooter," Zoe wrote in her biography about her husband. "Two were too heavy."[18]

While Bill was making a name for himself defending the law, Zoe remained at home at their ranch in Lincoln County, Oklahoma, writing. She penned such published works as *Sacajawea, The Shoshoni, Katska of the Seminoles,* and *Quanah the Eagle of the Comanche.* The latter book was the most well received of all the titles. She also authored western stories for periodicals such as *Lariat Story Magazine* and *Ranch Romance.*[19]

Zoe frequently wrote about her husband and the outlaws he apprehended. "He's given much of the credit for breaking up outlaw gangs that overran Oklahoma in the 1890s," she shared in articles she authored for the *Ada Evening News.* She bragged that he singlehandedly took in Bill Doolin, a gang leader who swore he wouldn't be taken alive, by beating Doolin to the draw. Tilghman was alone, too, when he captured Doolin's lieutenant, Little Bill Raidler. He outshot Raidler with a double-barrel shotgun.[20]

In addition to being a peace officer, Bill served in the Oklahoma Senate. He was active in the statehood movement and Democratic policies, helped organize the first state fair, and was an aide to many governors. By the time Bill was in his early seventies, he'd retired from law enforcement and was focusing on filmmaking. "He had a flair for making movies," Zoe remembered in her memoirs. Between 1908 and 1915, he made four westerns.[21]

In August 1924, against Zoe's objections, Bill came out of retirement to become city marshal of a booming Oklahoma oil town called Cromwell. It was here that he met his demise.

For a short while it appeared as if Marshal Tilghman was going to successfully reform the spot state investigators called "America's wildest town." An article on the front page of the *Manitowoc Herald News* described the scene:

> *Cromwell—paradise of the oilfield huskies, is being cleaned. In this town of 300 persons, state agents claim they found wide-open gambling, 200 dope peddlers, and many dance halls in which girls danced for 15 cents a dance to the tune of weird jazz music, and "choc" beer was sold. Hijackers, bootleggers, and suddenly rich oil men played for high stakes around the tables in clapboard huts. One out of every three houses in town was a home of ill fame, state investigators contend.[22]*
>
> *Federal officials have stepped in, drying up the town and breaking up the narcotic traffic. Then the governor and Judge Crump, backed by the businessmen, decided to hire Bill Tilghman as town marshal.*
>
> *Though Bill is along in years he is just as "hard" as he was in his younger days, the officials say. Bill has closed-up the saloons, a lot of the dance halls, and put the dope settlers on the run, in one week alone he and Deputy Sheriff Aldrich ushered 65 dancing girls out of town.[23]*

On November 1, 1924, a drunken Prohibition officer named Wiley Lynn shot and killed Bill. Bill suspected Lynn of being corrupt and was in the process of gathering evidence to arrest him when he was slain.

Lynn surrendered to authorities and admitted to the crime. He stood trial in federal court for the murder on May 20, 1925, and was acquitted. The jury found that his extreme drunkenness interfered with his judgment and exonerated him from the crime.[24]

Bill Tilghman was buried in Oak Park Cemetery in Chandler, Oklahoma. According to biographer Floyd Miller, "Zoe stood alone at his gravesite for a long while recalling the words her husband had spoken his last weekend home. She had urged him to set the date for his retirement and he had said, 'Other men will set that date.'"[25]

In tribute to her husband, Zoe wrote a book about the life of the intrepid, quick-drawing lawman in an almost lawless society. The book was entitled *Marshal of the Last Frontier: The Life and Service of William Matthew Tilghman*. Zoe died of natural causes in June 1964 and was buried next to Bill. She was almost eighty-four years old when she passed away.[26]

Love Lessons Learned by Calamity Jane

Understand that dressing like a man doesn't always mean you'll get your man. Calamity Jane learned this too late in life.

Be schooled in frontier social graces. Calamity Jane could outfight, out-cuss, and out-drink most men, and never got over the idea that these skills did not necessarily make her irresistible.

Never let your legendary status overshadow the legendary status of the one whose heart you hope to win. Calamity Jane had a habit of exaggerating her experiences on the frontier. Not only did her inflated reputation at times threaten to dwarf Hickok's, but it was intimidating to most men who hadn't accomplished as much and felt they had nothing unique to offer her.

Realize that the fact that you can drink a man under the table isn't a point of pride—at least not in the Old West. The way Calamity Jane staggered down the street after leaving a saloon left many men thinking that walking was a lost art to her.

Limit your profanity. Most men in the early days of the Old West lost interest in a woman who was skilled in the art of cursing. Some believed that St. Peter wouldn't accept women who used profanity regularly.

CALAMITY JANE

Love and the Legend

The town of Deadwood, South Dakota Territory, in 1876, was a mixture of makeshift tents erected by enthusiastic gold seekers, timber collectors, freight wagon owners, and owners of bawdy houses operated by some of the area's most notorious madams. Ribbed by thick, tree-filled mountain chains and bleak valleys, the popular mining camp was the ideal destination for eager prospectors hoping to find the mother lode.[1]

Shacks and lean-tos lined the muddy thoroughfare leading in and out of town. Livestock, including hogs and cattle, slogged through the muck and mire standing in the middle of Main Street. It was a primitive, unsanitary setting. Infrastructures and smooth roadways would come after gold was played out. Residents were more interested in finding a strike than building an orderly community.

The Black Hills District of Dakota, where Deadwood was located, was the last major gold field to be developed. In late 1875 prospectors had invaded the area and found rich placer diggings. The discovery was well publicized and started a stampede that brought hordes of miners into the region.[2]

Well-known western figures arrived on the scene hoping to capitalize on the lucrative gold business. Wild Bill Hickok, the most famous personality at the time, rode into town in July 1876 followed by an entourage that consisted of trappers, guides, gamblers, prospectors, Charlie "Colorado" Utter, Bill's brother Steve, and noted

Martha Jane Cannary, also known as "Calamity Jane," had a lifelong love for Wild Bill Hickok.

plainswoman Calamity Jane. Hickok was immediately recognized by the residents in the mining burg. His long hair, stallion-tail mustache, and more than six-foot-tall frame drew attention. His enormous cream-white Stetson crowned his flowing locks just right, and the butts of the revolvers he had tucked into a red sash tied around his waist gleamed in the lava-like sun.[3]

All of those riding with him were dressed in buckskin, including Calamity Jane. Miners roared with boisterous delight as the pageant slowly came to a stop in front of a saloon. Calamity Jane hopped off her mount and greeted the cheering crowd awaiting them. She shook hands with the prospectors and businessmen at the entrance of the saloon in a tough independent manner. Hickok hadn't known her long, but he knew she was in her element. She preferred the company of men and liked to drink a lot. Calamity Jane was more comfortable wearing the garb of a frontiersman and working occupations reserved for men.[4]

Wild Bill Hickok was amused by her unconventionalities, but her lack of femininity made it impossible for him to see her as anything other than one of the men that traveled with him. Calamity Jane, however, was completely taken by Hickok. Although she wore men's clothing, used colorful language, and drank to excess with male cohorts, beneath the rough exterior was the tender heart of a woman who ached to be in Hickok's constant presence. The fact that Hickok had married circus performer Agnes Lake in March 1876 and was deeply in love with his wife did not discourage Calamity Jane. In the weeks leading up to his death she rarely left his side.[5]

Calamity Jane was born in Princeton, Missouri, on May 1, 1852. She was the eldest of six children born to James and Charlotte Cannary and was given the name of Martha Jane. Shortly after Jane turned thirteen in 1865, her father moved the family to Virginia City, Montana, and began prospecting for gold. The trip west was difficult for the

Cannarys. The country was unsettled in many parts, and the only food available to the family was what they hunted and gathered for themselves. On this long journey, Calamity Jane learned how to become an expert horsewoman and to shoot game from atop her ride. She developed a love for the outdoor sport and the open range. By the time the Cannarys arrived in Montana, she was a master with a rifle and could drive a team of mules pulling a wagon.[6]

Within a few months of arriving in Virginia City, Calamity Jane's mother passed away. Unable to deal with the traumatic loss so far from the home the couple knew, Jane's father decided to return to Missouri. James became ill in Salt Lake City, Utah, and died, leaving Calamity Jane and her brothers and sister to fend for themselves.[7]

Calamity Jane found work on a ranch at Fort Bridger, Wyoming, and for a while managed to care for her siblings. Due to the kind of job she was given, she became even more proficient with a weapon and riding. Her reputation in that line of work grew throughout the territory. After a brief stay at Fort Bridger, Calamity Jane moved her family to Piedmont, Wyoming, where she was employed in a variety of odd jobs to support her siblings. She worked as a dishwasher, a cook, a waitress, a dance hall girl, nurse, and prostitute. Several months passed before Jane managed to find an occupation that she enjoyed above all others, that of an ox-team driver.[8]

According to her autobiography, Calamity Jane believed the time spent on the journey west helped set the stage for her unconventional way of earning a living. She recalled:

> *The trip west took five months to make, and I was at all times with men where there was excitement and adventure to be had. . . . I remember many occurrences on the journey. Many times in crossing the mountains, the conditions of the trail were so bad that*

we frequently had to lower the wagons over ledges by hand with ropes, for they were so rough and rugged that horses were of no use. We also had many exciting times fording streams, for many of the streams in our way were noted for quicksand and boggy places, where, unless we were very careful, we would have lost horse and all. Then we had many dangers to encounter in the way of swelling streams on account of heavy rains. On occasions of that kind, the men would usually select the best places to cross the streams; myself on more than one occasion, have mounted my pony and swam across the stream several times merely to amuse myself, and have had many narrow escapes from both myself and pony washed away to certain death . . . [9]

By the time Calamity Jane turned sixteen, the responsibility of caring for her brothers and sister had become too much for her to handle. Once she made sure her family had homes to go to, she set off on her own. The Union Pacific Railroad extended throughout the Wyoming territory enabling adventurous pioneers to travel easily from one military camp to the next. Believing there would be great job opportunities for her on the trail driving ox teams along the same route as the trains, Calamity Jane decided to visit the individual posts and the stops in between. She introduced herself and let everyone know she was a driver for hire. She looked forward to meeting new people at the posts, particularly men. [10]

Calamity Jane felt taking long rides over the plains and mountains, hunting, sleeping under the stars, drinking, smoking, playing cards, swimming in ponds and creeks, and cursing were easier to do with men than with prim and proper females who deemed such behavior unladylike. She was enchanted by men. Biographer Duncan Aikman noted that Calamity Jane always wanted men around and that "simply the distillation of their thronging maleness gave her exaltation." [11]

*Wild Bill Hickok arrived in Deadwood, South Dakota, with
Calamity Jane in 1876, but the two were not romantically involved.*

Adorned in buckskins and boots, Calamity Jane learned how to use a bullwhip and drove freight wagons loaded with timber from Fort Bridger to Fort Laramie. She hired on with hunting parties to acquire game for railroad workers and tried her hand at prospecting. The majority of men and women who came in contact with Calamity Jane were fascinated by her unique manner of dress and daring. Stories of the tough talking, rowdy lady had made their way around western communities and camps. Some tales reached as far east as New York. Proper women, ladies who conformed to conventional roles as wives and mothers, were horrified and angered by her outrageous behavior.[12]

By 1870, Jane had moved from Wyoming to Montana. The population of men had increased substantially in the area of Virginia City due to talk of gold being discovered in the area. As Jane preferred men over women, she decided to relocate. Wyoming had become too civilized for her tastes, overrun by women, children, and families who had finally joined their pioneering patriarchs. Virginia City was rowdy, and saloon-keepers and patrons there had no objection to Calamity Jane making herself comfortable at the bar and ordering drinks.[13]

It's hard to know how long Calamity Jane was in Virginia City and just where she ventured after her stay in the lawless mining camp. Newspaper records from the time note that she traveled back to Wyoming and on to Fort Russell. She had heard that General Armstrong Custer was at the post, and she wanted to meet him and persuade him to let her join him on his campaign against the Apache Indians in Arizona.[14] Some accounts have her reporting to General Crook at Fort Russell and hiring on as a scout.[15] Calamity Jane had a tendency to exaggerate her accomplishments and experiences and often got dates for certain events confused, making what actually happened and when difficult to decipher. Stretching the truth was another characteristic she shared with several men who frequented the same watering holes she did. Many historians agree that Calamity Jane was most likely in Deadwood, South Dakota, where she worked briefly as a bartender. She claimed there was an attempt to run her out of town by "the good virtuous women" of the community for maintaining such employment. They objected not only to a woman with that occupation but also to Calamity Jane's overall unkempt appearance. "They came into the saloon with a horsewhip and shears to cut off my hair," she recalled in her autobiography. "I jumped off the bar into their midst and before they could say 'sicken' I had them running."[16]

Calamity Jane drifted from the Dakotas back to Wyoming and followed Army General George R. Crook's men from Fort Russell to Arizona. According to the *Steubenville Herald* newspaper, Calamity Jane did serve as a scout for Crook during his time battling the Apache in Yavapai, Arizona, in 1872. Later she was transferred to a garrison near Goose Creek, Wyoming, and worked for Captain John Egan. It was while she was working as a scout that she received the name Calamity. Captain Egan's troops had been dispatched to deal with an uprising of Native Americans on their way back to camp. While en route, the soldiers were ambushed by the Indians. Captain Egan was shot and thrown from his ride. Calamity Jane noticed what had happened and without hesitating hurried out to rescue the officer. She pulled him onto her horse and brought him back to safety. Once the captain had recovered from the ordeal he told her, "I name you Calamity Jane, the heroine of the plains."[17]

Calamity Jane's fearlessness won her the respect of many men, but very few found her physically appealing. An intriguing description by one of her contemporaries goes: "Calamity had a shape like a hogshead with laigs [*sic*], and her face, which she seldom washed, was homely to the point of being plain revolting." A prospector acquaintance from Deadwood recorded in his memoirs that Calamity Jane's figure reminded him of a "busted bale of hay." Still another associate of the legend claimed that "a six-gun was served with each bottle of Red-Eye, for use if and when Calamity Jane began to look attractive."[18]

Calamity Jane's appreciation for the opposite sex did not waver with any insults she might have heard. No amount of criticism could persuade her to abandon the adventures she embarked on from Dodge City to Deadwood. According to the May 14, 1950, edition of the *Hutchinson News Herald*, "She lived life to the full and was known to Ellsworth, Abilene, Hays City, and all the army camps in Kansas, Nebraska and South Dakota."[19]

Calamity Jane was the epitome of the free western female. She was independent and completely uninhibited. Proof of her openness was exhibited in 1873 while in the company of a detachment of federal troops in the Black Hills of South Dakota. Dressed in an oversized army uniform, she accompanied troops on patrol. The party camped beside a stream one evening, and the soldiers decided to take a swim before turning in for the night. One of the officers strolling by the stream to watch the enlisted men paddling happily in the water got the jolt of his life. A naked Calamity Jane was in the water with the men. When the officer recovered from shock, Calamity Jane was sent back to Fort Laramie where the expedition originated. A strenuous effort was made to keep the incident quiet, but Calamity Jane was too proud of herself to not brag about the experience.[20]

Any man who assumed Calamity Jane was so unfeminine that one could make suggestive remarks to her in public was quickly corrected. She might have worn leather pants and a man's pullover woolen shirt and carried a pocket rifle, but that was no reason to think she wasn't a lady. Cowboy ballad singer Darling Bob Mackay learned that lesson the hard way one evening during a performance at the Comique Theatre in Dodge City, Kansas, in 1872.[21]

Calamity Jane was in the audience enjoying the show with a group of soldiers from a nearby fort when Darling Bob spotted her in the crowd. Bob had a talent for being risqué and decided to approach Calamity Jane with his daring act and put her on the spot. Loud enough for all to hear he asked her an intimate question about her lingerie. She was stunned and her voice filled the air with a shrill, obscene remark for his nerve, and she riddled the sombrero he was wearing for a costume with bullets. Calamity Jane then quickly left the performance demanding at gunpoint that her military escorts leave with her.[22]

Calamity Jane had acquired a taste for alcohol early in her life. It was not unusual for her to drink to excess, sing at the top of her lungs, pick fights with whomever was getting on her nerves, chew tobacco, and gamble. She was often jailed for drunk and disorderly conduct, and, according to *Sunset Magazine* reporter Lewis Freeman, she could seldom remember what transpired after such events.[23]

Few documented details exist on Calamity Jane's attempts at marriage, but she is rumored to have had more than one husband. Road agent and stage robber Duncan Blackburn was suspected as being one of them. South Dakota historians believe Calamity Jane helped him hold up three stages traveling from Cheyenne, Wyoming, to Deadwood. They are reported to have had a son together as well.[24]

Her desire to serve in the army, combined with the fact that she was "man crazy," as the *Hutchinson News Herald* reported in May 1950, continually drove Calamity Jane back to military posts in Wyoming and South Dakota. In early July 1876, after spending the night behind bars for drunk and disorderly conduct in Cheyenne, Calamity Jane headed to Fort Russell. The only thing she carried with her when she rode out of town was a bottle of whiskey. By the time she reached the post she was so blind drunk she couldn't see the place and rode right by it.[25]

Thinking the fort had been moved north of its original location, Calamity Jane continued riding on. She didn't stop until she reached the town of Chugwater, fifty miles away from Fort Russell. She decided to stay the night at a trading post and backtrack the following day.

After unloading her bedroll and unsaddling her horse, she made her way to a nearby saloon and proceeded to drink copious amounts of liquor. Calamity Jane remained at the bar until dawn. Before she left the saloon, the bartender refilled the whiskey bottle she'd brought with her the previous evening and warned her to "watch out for her scalp." She told the bartender that the "Indian who tried to get her scalp would never see daylight." Without any further word she hurried out of Chugwater in search of the missing fort.[26]

Late that afternoon she rode up to the gate at Fort Laramie, ninety miles from Cheyenne. The bottle of whiskey she'd been carrying with her was empty, and she was sober enough to realize the mistake she had made in relation to the fort. She was not disconcerted in the least. Fort Laramie was as welcome as Fort Russell would have been as long as the post trade store had plenty of whiskey.[27]

According to the July 27, 1876, edition of the *Helena Independent*, "Jane turned her horse out to grass and enjoyed camp life in her usual fashion until an officer came after her. It is not known whether Calamity Jane met any hostile Indians during her trip or not," the article noted. She said that she did. "A party of howling devils swooped down upon her and tried to capture her," she told a newspaper reporter, "but she swore at them until they left. The Sioux were probably awed by her profanity, or being exceedingly superstitious they may have taken Calamity Jane for Beelzebub himself, in the disguise of a Cheyenne beer jerker."[28]

Somewhere during her travels she met Wild Bill Hickok and was instantly enamored with him. They'd known each other only a short time before he was murdered on August 2, 1876, by Jack McCall.

97

Hickok's murder was a cruel one, and Calamity Jane was determined to bring the killer to justice. She claims to have been the one who had the honor of capturing McCall. "She did it with a butcher's cleaver, having left her rifle at home," the *Steubenville Herald* newspaper reported on February 26, 1896. "She made sure McCall passed over the great divide hanging to a limb of a cottonwood tree."[29]

Calamity Jane was heartbroken over Hickok's death, but took full advantage of his position to expand on their nonexistent physical relationship. After he had attained the status of dead hero, she cultivated an act for acquiring drinks when she went into a saloon. Calamity Jane would mourn loudly for Hickok until the heart of the bartender was softened into giving her a couple of drinks.[30]

Her association with Hickok, as well as her own much talked about western exploits, was the subject of a popular dime novel at the time. In 1901, after drinking all over the West for more than twenty years, she helped write an autobiography and put into print a collection of exaggerated half-truths and outrageous boasts.

One event she did not have to exaggerate or boast about occurred in 1878. A fearful smallpox epidemic had swept through the plains, and Calamity Jane worked night and day ministering to the ill and the dying. She went from shack to shack in the Deadwood area tending to the sick, handing out drugs she had bought herself, and preparing the dead for burial. Many pioneers owed Calamity Jane their lives in that year of horror in which she served as a tireless angel of mercy.[31]

Calamity Jane's drinking habit increased after Hickok was murdered. By the time she turned forty-nine in 1901, she was an alcoholic. She managed to stay sober long enough to appear in a few Wild West shows with Buffalo Bill Cody at the Pan-American Exposition in New York. Calamity Jane was billed as the "famous woman scout." The drinking binges she embarked on eventually cost her any performing jobs. Homeless and destitute, Calamity Jane ended up working at a house of ill repute in Montana. Sick and intoxicated, she spurned any attempt to help her get well. "Leave me alone and let me go to hell my own route," she barked to well-meaning friends.[32]

On August 1, 1903, the "Heroine of the Whoop-Up," as the dime novels referred to her, died in Terry, South Dakota. Those around her when she passed said she left this life calling out Bill Hickok's name and insisting she be buried next to "the only man she ever loved."[33]

The remains of Calamity Jane were placed in Mount Moriah Cemetery in Deadwood beside the bones of Wild Bill Hickok. According to the *Black Hills Daily Times,* Jane's funeral was one of the largest Deadwood had ever seen. Mourners paraded past her casket, remembering with fondness Calamity Jane's character. One resident, who felt that the once-feisty woman lying in state dressed in a white cotton dress did not look natural, placed a six-shooter in each hand. The undertaker removed the weapons and chastised viewers about disturbing the body. His pleas went ignored and many in attendance cut locks of her hair off to keep as souvenirs. The man was finally forced to build a wire cage over the corpse to prevent further action.[34]

Friends who spoke at Calamity Jane's funeral said she was a "woman of the world with an independence of character" and "the mistress of her own destiny." Many of her male friends claimed she was the "original frontier terror" and swore that "her face wouldn't have looked good on a Gila monster."[35]

Love Lessons Learned
by Geronimo's Wives

Know that no one can fully take the place of that first, true love. Geronimo had several wives, but none he loved as much as his first, Alope. He spent much of his life trying to avenge her death.

Be willing to live and die for the man you love. Women who married the defiant Geronimo after he had lost other wives in raids on Apache encampments must have believed the risk was worth it.

Learn to love an intrepid life. Geronimo warred against the men who killed his family and threatened to destroy his way of life. Oftentimes his family was with him as he chased his enemy from western location to western location.

Surrender to escaping with your husband. Geronimo eventually resolved to go to a reservation, but he didn't stay. Wives and children often went with him when he'd had enough of captivity.

Keep his memory alive. Geronimo's wives passed on to their children stories of their life with the charismatic Apache warrior who refused to give in against all odds. His memory lives on today.

GERONIMO'S WIVES

Love and the Indian Chief

Seventeen-year-old Geronimo rode quickly out of a rocky canyon near Clifton in southern Arizona, chasing half a dozen wild horses. The animals' hooves pounded hard into the parched earth, leaving dusty impressions behind. It was desperately hot, and foam flecks of sweat bounced off their backs, evaporating into the air before having a chance to dot the arid landscape. The horses showed no signs of slowing down and neither did the teenage rider following them. Geronimo's face was a study of relentless purpose. Horses and rider had traveled a long way and now raced through scrub and brush toward an encampment of Bedonkohe Apache Indians. The cloud of dust kicked up by Geronimo and the animals in front of him did not escape the attention of several members of the tribe. They squinted against the glare of the ruddy sunset to take in the sight.[1]

Geronimo brought the horses to an easy pace as he neared the camp, pushed them to the dwelling of No-po-so, and dismounted. No-po-so was the father of Alope, the woman Geronimo loved and wanted to marry. It wasn't until after the young Apache Indian was admitted to the council of warriors and had presented his future father-in-law with a number of horses that Geronimo and Alope could be husband and wife. The wedding ceremony itself was the simple act of relinquishing the horses to No-po-so.[2]

Apache war chief Geronimo at the age of seventy-eight

Germonimo and his bride made their home near his mother's wickiup. According to Geronimo, Alope was "slender and fair, loyal and dutiful." The two had been lovers for a long time, and he considered marrying her to be the "greatest joy offered to him." The pair wed in 1846 and resided in a wickiup made of buffalo hides. The interior of their home was filled with bear and lion robes, spears, bows, and arrows. Alope decorated their dwelling with beadwork and elaborate drawings made on buckskin. Her artistry extended onto the canvas walls of the wickiup as well.[3]

Geronimo boasted in his autobiography entitled *Geronimo, His Own Story,* that Alope was a good wife. They followed the traditions of their forefathers and were very happy. During the first few years of their married life, Alope bore Geronimo three sons. "Children that played, loitered, and worked as I had done," Geronimo later recalled of his family.[4]

In 1858, Geronimo took his wife and sons and traveled from his camp with other Apache tribesmen and their families to Chihuahua to trade items for supplies that were needed. The journey from Janos into the Mexican state was something the Apache Indians did once a year. The tribe set up camp outside the town of Janos, and the men made the trip to the northern Mexico location to do business with general stores willing to trade with them. It was during one of the visits to Janos that the Apache encampment was attacked by Mexican troops who considered the Indians to be intruders in their territory. Many of the Apache women, children, and elderly were slaughtered and scalped. In addition to the murders of the defenseless Indians, Mexican soldiers seized all the supplies and weapons from the wickiups.[5]

Geronimo and the other members of the council of warriors with him were horrified by the sight. Among the dead were Alope, Geronimo's sons, and his mother. The Mexicans had cut off the victims' hair, and the ground was saturated with their blood. "I stood hardly knowing what I would do," Geronimo shared in his autobiography. "I had no weapon, nor did I hardly wish to fight, neither did I contemplate recovering the bodies of my loved ones, for that was forbidden. I did not pray, nor did I resolve to do anything in particular for I had no purpose left."[6]

Geronimo grieved over the loss of his family as he followed his tribe out of the area. He didn't eat, sleep, or speak to anyone for three days. When he finally talked, he spoke only of the massacre and the Mexican troops who were now his enemies. He returned to the home he and Alope had shared with their boys and was quickly assaulted by the memory of them all around him. "There were decorations that Alope had made," he recalled later in his life, "and there were playthings of our little ones." Geronimo burned the wickiup that belonged to him and his wife along with all their personal items. He did the same thing to his mother's home and possessions. He vowed revenge upon Mexico and the troopers who had wronged him. Thus began the rise of the man some historians refer to as a "savage of the worst stripe."[7]

Geronimo was married more than nine times, but the loss of his first wife had a profound effect on him. His first act of retaliation for the murder of his family occurred in mid-1859 when he joined the Chiricahua tribe of Apaches in a series of deadly raids on Sonora. "I could not call back my loved ones, but I could rejoice in revenge," he noted in his autobiography.[8]

Geronimo was born on June 16, 1829, and was crowned chief of the Chiricahuas before he turned twenty. He became one of the most feared and tenacious of the North American Indians. His boldness in battle and sharp intellect made for admirable qualities in not only a leader, but also a husband. He was offered the hand of many Apache women. He selected a beautiful Bedonkohe woman named Chee-hash-kish to be his second wife. Geronimo and Chee-hash-kish had two children, Dohn-say and Chappo.[9]

It is not known how long after Alope was slain that Geronimo wed Chee-hash-kish, but in times of war it was considered acceptable by the Apache to marry quickly and often. The concern that warriors would die in battle without an heir was great. Indian maidens required strong men to provide for them as well. They needed items, such as food and horses, retrieved from raids on various settlements to survive.[10]

Nana-Tha-Thtith became Geronimo's third wife. She was killed by Mexican soldiers in 1861. Geronimo was recovering from a gunshot wound when the renegade troops rushed into his camp. He had little time to arm himself before the troops descended upon him and members of his tribe. Even with his injury, he managed to kill many soldiers, but it came too late to save Nana-Tha-Thtith and the child she had. No mention is made in Geronimo's autobiography that the child belonged to him. Speculation is that her husband had died in a previous battle and Geronimo assumed the role of father.[11]

By the time Geronimo married again, white settlers had invaded Apache land, and he was warring against the intrusion. She-gha was Geronimo's fourth wife. She was related to Cochise, chief of the Chokonen band of Chiricahua Apache. Not long after marrying She-gha, he wed another Bedonkohe woman named Shtsha-she.[12]

In 1863, Mangas Colorado, chief of the Warm Springs Chiricahua and the leader Geronimo served under as a warrior, was killed, and Geronimo became head of the tribe. Mangas Colorado had believed he could peacefully persuade white settlers to leave Apache land. Geronimo disagreed. Mangas Colorado was taken captive by US troops, shot, and then decapitated. The inhumane treatment of the respected chief further outraged Geronimo and added another slain person to the list he sought to avenge. He led several warriors into battle, which resulted in the death of many more Apache Indians, pioneers, and US soldiers. His resentment of Mexicans was unrelenting. He continued to lead

Ta-ayz-slath was one of Geronimo's wives. The boy beside her is Geronimo's son.

raiding parties on Mexican villages and camps more than twenty years after Alope was murdered.[13]

In 1882, Chee-hash-kish was taken by Mexican troops who hated the Apache Indians and Geronimo. She was sold as a slave and no one ever heard from her or about her again. After losing Chee-hash-kish, Geronimo took two more wives, Ta-ayz-slath and Zi-yeh. Not much is known about Ta-ayz-slath, but Zi-yeh was a Nednai Indian, and her father was a white man. Zi-yeh had been raised by a white family. She had a son named Fenton whom Geronimo helped to raise, and together he and Zi-yeh had two children, a son and a daughter.[14]

Frustrated with the fact that Geronimo would not surrender and agree to live on a reservation, the US government decided to crush the Indian leader for good in 1883. The rebel force he led was dedicated to fighting against anyone who tried to force them off their ancestral land and committed to vindicating the death of any Apache killed by Mexican troops. Mexican troops were blamed for the death of Shtsha-she and Geronimo's son. They died after a raid on a Mexican ranch in early 1883.[15] Among Geronimo's principle followers were twenty-six warriors and seventy women and children. Although unquestionably loyal to Geronimo, many of the Apache Indians with him were weary and demoralized. A full year would pass before he would relent and allow US soldiers to escort him to the reservation in Arizona's White Mountains. During that time his wives Zi-yeh and She-gha and five of his children had been captured by US troops. He was later reunited with them at the government run camp.[16]

Geronimo tried for a year to live in peace on the reservation, but tensions were mounting within the Apache settlement. Food rations designated for the Apache were not delivered or were rotten and moldy when they arrived. Indian warriors who had provided for their families by hunting game were forced to become farmers.

On May 17, 1885, Geronimo left the reservation with 145 others. Among that number were Geronimo's wives and his children. On their escape into Mexico, Geronimo's band killed seventeen white people. The battle to recapture the Apache chief was bitter. Geronimo's wife Zi-yeh and her daughter were recaptured on September 22, 1885, and brought back to the White Mountain reservation.[17]

Geronimo then married a woman traveling with him named In-tedda, also known as Kate Cross Eyes, and adopted her eleven-year-old son. As they fled from the soldiers and camped in the Sierra Madre Mountains, Geronimo taught the youngster how to be a warrior. Geronimo and his adopted son defended themselves and their camp from US and Mexican troops hoping to overtake them.[18]

After more than a year on the run, the Apache fugitives were desperate to see their families and relatives again. This prompted Geronimo to surrender on September 4, 1886.[19]

An article that appeared in the July 2, 1886, edition of the Spirit Lake, Iowa, newspaper, the *Spirit Lake Beacon*, described how the Apaches who had chosen not to follow Geronimo had been living under government authority at the White Mountain reservation. "Women and children have happily partaken of the United States hospitality," the article read. "All are blessed with sufficient freedom. The youngsters romped outside at will and the squaws adorned the porch of the guard house daily. They are a rather industrious set and turn many a proper peso by weaving handsome baskets of bear-grass, making moccasins for the soldiers, and constructing toy models of their unique candles. They were also given some light work to do around the post, which helped to keep them healthy and happy."[20]

Geronimo disputed claims that the Indians were happy and healthy on a reservation. He longed to be with his wives and children only mildly more than he longed to be free. The federal government did not extend any of the amenities to Geronimo and his followers they boasted were given to other captives. For their intransigent resistance, the Chiricahua chief and his loyal few were punished as no other US Indian had been. All of them, even women and children, ultimately served thirty years as prisoners of war—first in Florida and Alabama, then at Fort Sill in Oklahoma.[21]

Geronimo was considered an old man by the time he was transported by government officials to Florida. The fifty-seven-year-old was described by the September 27, 1886, edition of the Galveston, Texas, newspaper, *Galveston News,* as a "5'9" man weighing one hundred eighty-six pounds. . . . His figure is straight as the barrel of his own Winchester and were his face not considerably drawn he would show no signs of age," the article continued. "His eyes are small, black, and bright. His hair is long, black, and glossy. It is carefully combed down on each side of his face. Many Apache Indian women, even those he had been married to for a long period of time, looked at him with admiration."[22]

While riding home from the town of Lawton, Oklahoma, on a wintry night in 1909, Geronimo fell off his horse and lay in a ditch until the morning. By the time friends found the aged chief, he was suffering with a bad chest cold. He died on February 17, 1909, from pneumonia. On his deathbed, he spoke the names of his warriors who had stayed loyal to the end, of his children, and his wife Alope.[23]

With the exception of Alope, all of Geronimo's wives died in captivity. Kate Cross Eyes survived the longest. She passed away in July 1950. She had been captured by US soldiers in 1886 and imprisoned at St. Augustine, Florida, and Mount Vernon, Alabama. She was later moved to the Mescalero reservation in New Mexico. She was ninety-four when she died.[24]

Love Lessons Learned
by Eleanora Dumont

Choose your profession wisely. Some men didn't mind
being seen with a lady card dealer at a gambling hall
in the evening, but most didn't want to be seen with a
woman in that profession in public during the day.

Understand that your unique talents may not be embraced
by men. Gambling in the Old West was considered a
man's job opportunity, and out-of-work poker dealers
didn't take kindly to Eleanora's skill. Some might have
even hated her for it.

Beware of handsome card players who flatter their way
into your heart and bank account. "It only makes your
luck run kind of muddy," prospectors in 1850 used to say.

Know that drinking yourself to an early grave won't win
the heart of the man you love. "It's like playing a harp
with a hammer," was another saying prospectors in the
mid-1800s used.

Keep up with your grooming habits. A mustache on a
woman isn't as well received as on a cowboy. Eleanora's
reign as the Queen of Twenty-One came to an end when
men began to make fun of her fading beauty.

ELEANORA DUMONT

Love and the Journalist

On June 15, 1853, a vivacious, petite woman stepped cheerfully off a stagecoach in Nevada City, California, dressed with all the style of Princess Eugenia of Sweden and Norway. As she strolled into the National Hotel with her dainty steps and her bustle looping back and forth, she made a decision to change her name from Mademoiselle Simone Jules (the handle she used when she first arrived in California in 1850) to Madame Eleanora Dumont. She wanted a new sobriquet to go with the new gambling hall she had opened in the booming gold-mining town. At the time it was unheard of for a woman to enter into such a business venture alone, but Madame Dumont was defiant and confident she would be successful. Champagne and food were free at her place and the girls she employed more lovely than any west of the Rockies.[1]

Eleanora's gambling hall was filled to overflowing every night. Her specialty was dealing Twenty-one or Blackjack. In her flinty, sing-song voice, she would invite card players to "have a go" at *vingt-et-un*, the French translation of the game. Patrons were so busy talking with the charming Madame Dumont during the round that they scarcely noticed when they'd lost. Losers who were good sports were treated like royalty by the women who worked in Eleanora's brothel. Keeping customers in good humor despite losing their money ensured repeat business. When she had to pay off she did so with a careless, come-on laugh. Hundreds of miners came to inspect the novelty of a beautiful lady gambler and stayed because they had a better time at the "Madams" than at other gambling joint.[2]

According to the July 6, 1859, edition of the *Logansport Journal,*

Eleanora learned her trade in London. There was more gambling among women at the time than had been the case since public gambling tables were put down by act of Parliament. The harmless bet of a few pairs of gloves at race meetings is now considered far beneath the notice of a dashing matron or fast maiden. There are but few female "plungers" on the turf who "put the pot on," as the idiotic jargon of the race course has it, with as much eagerness as the broke subaltern at the Raleigh, who stands to win a heap of money at Ascot or at Goodwood, with the alternative of running his old father, the country rector, if he loses, and allow his sisters' portions to be swallowed up in paying for his "debts of honor." If the female plunger be unmarried she has resource probably to some accommodating dressmaker, or, worse still, she accepts pecuniary help from some male friend, and perhaps puts herself for life in the power of a man who will one day make her pay dearly for her indiscretion.[3]

Eleanora was twenty years old when she moved to San Francisco from Europe. She took a job right away as a croupier for the roulette game at the Bella Union saloon. From there she traveled to Nevada City where in a short time she amassed considerable capital.[4]

When Eleanora wasn't dealing at her Nevada City gambling hall, she mingled with the rowdy clientele, flirting and flattering, rolling cigarettes and pouring drinks. Outside of her business, Madame Dumont conducted herself with the utmost propriety. She was always appropriately dressed, polite, and careful never to appear snobbish or withdrawn. She graciously declined the advances of amorous miners who hoped to "make an honest woman" out of her. Her evenings were spent alone in her hotel room.[5]

Eleanora Dumont, aka Madam Mustache, was unafraid to use her pistol to defend herself.

Nevada County historians note that the sophisticated Eleanora harbored a deep love for Editor Waite of the *Nevada Journal*. She adored him and longed for the respectability that he offered. Waite, however, did not return Eleanora's affections. There were occasional late-night calls to her room, but outside of fulfilling a basic need, Waite had no further use for her. The ultimate demise of their relationship came after Waite married a "socially acceptable" woman. Eleanora would never get over the loss.[6]

Rumors of gold being played out in the region began circulating in early 1855. Prospectors slowly filtered out of the mining town. Eleanora's business suffered as a result. The decrease in revenue, combined with the sadness she continued to feel over Editor Waite's marriage, left her vulnerable, both professionally and emotionally. Enter Lucky Dave Tobin. Tobin, a tall man with devilish good looks, was an itinerate gambler. Not long after introducing himself to the French beauty, he persuaded her to take him on as a partner in her struggling establishment. Tobin immediately began making improvements. He added keno tables, roulette wheels, and a faro bank. Dumont's place flourished once again.[7]

The relationship between Eleanora and Tobin eventually became more than business. As their romance flourished, the percentage he made from her gambling hall increased. Their partnership dissolved when Tobin demanded a bigger cut of the income than Eleanora was willing to give. In a heated discussion one evening, she informed him that she didn't need a man. She had gotten along fine prior to his assistance and would do so again. The partners went their separate ways.[8]

Tobin took his huge stash of earned profits and headed to New York. According to an article in the December 9, 1928, edition of the *Oakland Tribune*, Tobin opened his own gambling house there. Between 1862 and 1865, Tobin made thousands of dollars in card games he played with Civil War profiteers and successful politicians. Tobin died in 1865; what became of the money he had remains a mystery.[9]

Eleanora did not stay in Nevada City long after Tobin walked out of her life. In 1856, news of the rich Comstock Lode in Nevada reached the mining community, and Eleanora decided to go where money could be made. She sold the business and decided to follow the various gold and silver strikes throughout the West. She was always a mining camp favorite and never failed to draw a crowd. Prior to Editor Waite's betrayal, she had always been a temperate wine drinker. When she realized all hope of having him in her life was lost, she began consuming whiskey and brandy on a regular basis. Her drinking increased substantially once she began traveling from one Gold Rush town to another. For a while, Eleanora became careless at the gambling tables because of her drinking, and her winnings decreased. Her presence in mining towns like Columbia, California, threatened gamblers who had established those spots. The criticism she received about her drinking, followed by a strong suggestion she leave the area, further enhanced her alcohol intake.[10]

From Columbia she moved to Idaho, stopping off long enough in gold mining towns like Orofino, Florence, and Boise City to win large sums of money. She used her winnings to purchase other gambling houses. One such place was in Virginia City, Nevada. While she was there some of her old gaiety seemed to return. She started a riot at the gambling hall one evening after soundly beating a popular prospector at poker. Several of the prospector's friends, intent on getting the miner's money back that he had lost, started after her. She slowly backed up against one of the walls in the hall and started kidding the rowdy crowd. Other patrons who had known Eleanora for years and were witness to the ruckus told Virginia City newspaper reporters that her wit again sparked and there was a flash in her eyes. "For a brief moment it almost seemed some of the heartache she had known since the hour Editor Waite married another had faded," the article in the December 19, 1858, edition of the *Territorial Enterprise* read.[11]

By 1864, she was sharing her talents with argonauts in Bannack, Montana. She purchased a fancy, two-story place that had a saloon downstairs and a brothel upstairs. Among the many young women who worked to keep the miners' winnings in the house was a fifteen-year-old girl named Martha Jane Cannary. Martha Jane, better known as Calamity Jane, was one of the Wild West's most notorious characters.[12]

Madame Dumont's time in any one place was brief. After her stay in Bannack, she moved on to Bozeman, then to Fort Benton. In 1867,

Eleanora Dumont, aka Simone Jules. Madam
Mustache was California's first lady card
shark.

she added railroad construction camps to her itinerary of stopovers. She followed the Union Pacific workers throughout Wyoming and back to Nevada.[13]

Historical records indicate that somewhere on her journey, between 1865 and 1868, she met, married, and divorced a cattle buyer named Jack McKnight. The pair settled on a ranch near Carson City, Nevada, and for a while they were happy. The blissful union ended when McKnight abruptly left, taking all of Eleanora's money with him. Alone and destitute, she was forced back into a life of gambling and prostitution.[14]

Eleanora now began drinking heavily. Lines of grief and desperation marred her beautiful face. Her features coarsened, and a growth of dark hair appeared on her upper lip. Unsympathetic men she encountered in towns and camps ridiculed her looks and conferred upon her the title of "Madame Moustache." Although she tried to hide it, the handle cut deeply.[15]

In 1867, Eleanora returned to San Francisco, where her career had begun, and opened another parlor house. Her excessive drinking had affected her skill at cards, but patrons continued to seek her out and challenge her to games. She still managed to win the majority of hands, and most maintained that they "would rather lose to Madame Dumont than win from any male tin horn."[16]

Not everyone appreciated Eleanora's notoriety. Some men resented being taken by a woman at cards and looked forward to the day when her career would end and she would leave town altogether. In the fall of 1869, she did leave San Francisco, and stage magician John Henry Anderson remarked: "Mlle. Dumont has apparently gone out of business. I was told that early this morning carriages took the ladies and their baggage, and shortly after dinner the proprietress was seen departing, without a word to anyone, as perhaps fitting. A man came later this afternoon and took those two loads of chairs, but not the beds."[17]

After departing San Francisco, Eleanora headed back to Montana, where she frequented such locations as Virginia City and Last Chance Gulch. From there she took her business back to Idaho and towns like Murray, Coeur d'Alene, and Eagle City, then on to Deadwood, South Dakota, and Cheyenne, Wyoming. At each stop Eleanora kept an eye out for her ex-husband, Jack McKnight. Her pistol was always close at hand in case she saw him. She promised herself that if their paths ever crossed, she'd put a bullet in the man who had stolen her heart and her money.[18]

At the age of fifty, her card-playing talents and beauty fading and her once petite figure now overweight, Eleanora decided to move her game to Bodie, California. A gold strike there had made the tough northern California camp a popular destination for ambitious miners.[19]

Eleanora arrived in the bustling town in September of 1879. After enjoying more than a few drinks at one of the thirty saloons in the small town, Eleanora staggered over to a Twenty-One table and began playing. By the end of the evening, she had lost all of her money.[20]

Sitting in the back of the Grand Central Saloon, Eleanora contemplated how far she'd come from the profitable days she had once enjoyed in Nevada City. She thought about all she had lost, and her mind settled on Editor Waite. She sunk into a deep depression. The bartender offered her a bottle of whiskey, and she didn't refuse. Maybe she could drink her memories away.[21]

On the morning of September 8, Eleanora's dead body was found outside town. An empty vial of poison was discovered nearby, and clutched in her hand was a tear-stained note requesting that she be buried next to Editor Waite. Newspapers across the West posted the famous gambler's obituary, graciously omitting from their report the cruel nickname of Madame Moustache. The *Sacramento Union* reported: "A woman named Eleanor [*sic*] Dumont was found dead today about one mile out of town, having committed suicide. She was well known through all the mining camps. Let her many good qualities invoke leniency in criticizing her failings."[22]

Bodie townspeople and saloon owners took up a collection for Eleanora's burial. They were able to raise money to bury her in Bodie and would not allow her to be laid to rest in the "outcast cemetery."[23]

NOTES

Agnes Lake

1. *Tribune,* August 29, 1929.

2. Roberts, Phil. *Agnes Thatcher Lake: Equestrian Rider, Circus Performer, and Wild Bill's Wife.* Department of History, University of Wyoming, Laramie, WY, 2007. Fielder, Mildred. *Wild Bill & Deadwood.* Superior Publishing Company, Seattle, WA, 1965, pg. 65-68.

3. *Tribune,* August 29, 1929.

4. Ibid.

5. Ibid.

6. Ibid.

7. Ibid.

8. Ibid.

9. Roberts, Phil. *Agnes Thatcher Lake: Equestrian Rider, Circus Performer, and Wild Bill's Wife.* Department of History, University of Wyoming, Laramie, WY, 2007. Rosa, Joseph. *They Called Him Bill.* University of Oklahoma, Norman, OK, 1964, pg. 235-238. Fisher, Linda. *Agnes Lake Hickok: Queen of the Circus, Wife of a Legend.* University of Oklahoma, Norman, OK, 2009, pg. 113-119.

10. Ibid. *New York Times,* August 23, 1907

11. Roberts, Phil. *Agnes Thatcher Lake: Equestrian Rider, Circus Performer, and Wild Bill's Wife.* Department of History, University of Wyoming, Laramie, WY, 2007. Fielder, Mildred. *Wild Bill & Deadwood.* Superior Publishing Company, Seattle, WA, 1965, pg. 65-68.

12. *Cedar Rapids Evening Gazette,* September 3, 1907. *Hawk-Eye,* August 29, 1965.

13. *Cheyenne Daily Leader,* March 7, 1876. Fisher, Linda. *Agnes Lake Hickok: Queen of the Circus, Wife of a Legend.* University of Oklahoma, Norman, OK, 2009, pg. 113-119. *Galveston News,* January 22, 1907.

14. Ibid.

15. *New York Times,* August 23, 1907. *Cedar Rapids Evening Gazette,* September 3, 1907.

16. Fielder, Mildred. *Wild Bill & Deadwood.* Superior Publishing Company, Seattle, WA, 1965, pg. 65-68. Crutchfield, James A., Bill O'Neal, and Dale L. Walker. *Legends of the Wild West.* Publications International, Ltd., Lincolnwood, IL, 1995, pg. 106-108.

17. *Tribune,* August 29, 1929. *New York Times,* August 23, 1907. *Hays Daily News,* August 1, 2001.

18. Fielder, Mildred. *Wild Bill & Deadwood.* Superior Publishing Company, Seattle, WA, 1965, pg. 65-68. *Tribune,* August 29, 1929.

19. Ibid.

20. Ibid.

21. Rezatto, Helen. *Tales of the Black Hills.* Fenwyn Press, Rapid City, SD, 1989, pg. 64, 85, 185.

22. Ibid. *Hays Daily News,* August 1, 2001. *Sioux City Sunday Journal,* July 12, 1925.

23. *Tribune,* August 29, 1929. Fielder, Mildred. *Wild Bill & Deadwood.* Superior Publishing Company, Seattle, WA, 1965, pg. 65-68.

24. *Black Hills Pioneer,* August 2, 1876.

25. *Soda Springs News,* September 8, 1877. Fielder, Mildred. *Wild Bill & Deadwood.* Superior Publishing Company, Seattle, WA, 1965, pg. 77-82. Nash, Jay R. *Encyclopedia of Western Lawmen & Outlaws.* Paragon House, New York, NY, 1992, pg. 155-159.

26. *Tribune,* August 29, 1929.

27. Fielder, Mildred. *Wild Bill & Deadwood.* Superior Publishing Company, Seattle, WA, 1965, pg. 103-111. Nash, Jay R. *Encyclopedia*

of Western Lawmen & Outlaws. Paragon House, New York, NY, 1992, pg. 155-159.

28. *New York Times*, August 22, 1907.

Etta Place

1. *American Weekly,* February 10, 1950. Nash, Jay R. *Encyclopedia of Western Lawmen & Outlaws.* Paragon House, New York, NY, 1992, pg. 68-71. *Idaho State Journal,* August 27, 1976.

2. Ibid. *Washington Post,* July 7, 1907. *Atlanta Journal Constitution,* July 8, 1904. *The News Magazine Supplement, Cleveland Sun News,* February 19, 1929.

3. *Washington Post,* July 7, 1907. Alexander, Kent. *Legends of the Old West.* Friedman/Fairfax Publishers, New York, NY, 1994, pg. 66-69. *Atlanta Journal Constitution,* July 3, 1904.

4. *American Weekly,* February 10, 1950. Alexander, Kent. *Legends of the Old West.* Friedman/Fairfax Publishers, New York, NY, 1994, pg. 66-69. Nash, Jay R. *Encyclopedia of Western Lawmen & Outlaws.* Paragon House, New York, NY, 1992, pg. 68-71. *Idaho State Journal,* August 27, 1976.

5. *Washington Post,* July 7, 1907. *San Antonio Light,* December 19, 1917.

6. *Idaho State Journal,* August 27, 1976. *American Weekly,* February 10, 1950. *Des Moines News,* August 12, 1918. Nash, Jay R. *Encyclopedia of Western Lawmen & Outlaws.* Paragon House, New York, NY, 1992, pg. 68-71.

7. *Seattle Post Intelligencer,* September 18, 1920.

8. *Courier News,* July 31, 1975.

9. Kirby, Edward. *The Saga of Butch Cassidy and the Wild Bunch.* Filter Press, Denver, CO, 1977 pg. 41-42.

10. *Courier News,* July 31, 1975. *San Antonio Light,* December 19, 1917. Rutter, Michael. *Wild Bunch Women.* TwoDot, Guilford, CT, 2003, pg. 53-62.

11. *San Antonio Light,* December 19, 1917.

12. Nash, Jay R. *Encyclopedia of Western Lawmen & Outlaws.* Paragon House, New York, NY, 1992, pg. 68-71. *Washington Post,* July 7, 1907. Wilson, Gary. A *Tiger of the Wild Bunch.* TwoDot, Guilford, CT, 2007, pg. 1-5.

13. *American Weekly,* February 10, 1950. *Idaho State Journal,* August 27, 1976.

14. *Courier News,* July 31, 1975. Nash, Jay R. *Encyclopedia of Western Lawmen & Outlaws.* Paragon House, New York, NY, 1992, pg. 68-71.

15. *Courier News,* July 31, 1975. Crutchfield, James A., Bill O'Neal, and Dale L. Walker. *Legends of the Wild West.* Publications International, Ltd., Lincolnwood, IL, 1995, pg. 300-305. Burton, Doris K. *Queen Ann Bassett Alias Etta Place.* Burton Enterprises, Fayetteville, TN, 1992, pg. 44-47.

16. Crutchfield, James A., Bill O'Neal, and Dale L. Walker. *Legends of the Wild West.* Publications International, Ltd., Lincolnwood, IL, 1995, pg. 300-305. Alexander, Kent. *Legends of the Old West.* Friedman/Fairfax Publishers, New York, NY, 1994, pg. 66-69.

17. *American Weekly,* February 10, 1950. Nash, Jay R. *Encyclopedia of Western Lawmen & Outlaws.* Paragon House, New York, NY, 1992, pg. 68-71. *Idaho State Journal,* August 27, 1976.

18. *San Antonio Light,* December 19, 1917.

19. *Los Angeles Times,* April 7, 1970.

20. Burton, Doris K. *Queen Ann Bassett Alias Etta Place.* Burton Enterprises, Fayetteville, TN, 1992, pg. 44-47.

21. *San Antonio Light,* December 19, 1917.

NOTES

22. *American Weekly,* February 10, 1950. Rutter, Michael. *Wild Bunch Women.* TwoDot, Guilford, CT, 2003, pg. 53-62. *Idaho State Journal,* August 27, 1976. *Daily Democrat Times,* April 7, 1970.

Emma Walter

1. *New York Clipper*, January 17, 1891. Penn, Chris. "Bat Masterson's Emma," *Wild West Magazine,* April 2012.
2. *Sandusky Daily Register,* January 15, 1891. McWhirter, Norris. *Guinness Book of World Records,* 1997 Edition. Bantam Publishing, New York, NY, 1997, pg. 467. *Encyclopedia Britannica,* Robert Fitzsimmons, Encyclopedia Britannica, Inc., 2000, pg. 42.
3. *New York Clipper,* January 17, 1891. *Sandusky Daily Register,* January 15, 1891.
4. Ibid.
5. *New York Clipper,* January 17, 1891.
6. *Berkshire Eagle,* November 4, 1958. Ancestry.com, Emma Walter.
7. Ancestry.com, Edwin Moulton. *New York Times,* April 17, 1893. *New York Times*, March 19, 1935.
8. Ancestry.com, Edwin Moulton.
9. Penn, Chris. "Bat Masterson's Emma," *Wild West Magazine,* April 2012. Breihan, Carl W. "They Call Him 'Bat,'" *Old Timers Wild West,* October 1978, No. 4.
10. Ancestry.com, Edwin Moulton.
11. Miller, Frank E. *Indian Club Swinging.* University of California Libraries, San Diego, CA, 1900.
12. Ibid.
13. Montgomery Ward Co. pamphlet, Chicago, IL, 1886. Penn, Chris. "Bat Masterson's Emma," *Wild West Magazine,* April 2012.

14. *Daily Free Press,* October 13, 1879. *New York Clipper,* October 7, 1882. Houseworth, Thomas. *Tony Denier, the Celebrated Pantomimist.* Yale Books, New Haven, CT, 1910.

15. Ibid. *New York Clipper,* October 7, 1882. *New York Clipper,* October 28, 1879. Ancestry.com, Clifton family.

16. *Chicago Daily Tribune,* August 17, 1879.

17. Penn, Chris. "Bat Masterson's Emma," *Wild West Magazine,* April 2012.

18. *Rocky Mountain News,* April 21, 1884. *Rocky Mountain News,* March 15, 1889.

19. Ibid.

20. Penn, Chris. "Bat Masterson's Emma," *Wild West Magazine,* April 2012. DeArment, Robert K. *Bat Masterson: The Man and the Legend.* University of Oklahoma Press, Norman, OK, 1979, pg. 325.

21. Ibid., pg. 37-48. *Mills County Tribune,* August 29, 1895. Breihan, Carl W. "They Call Him 'Bat,'" *Old Timers Wild West,* October 1978, No. 4.

22. Ibid.

23. *Register News,* August 22, 1958. DeArment, Robert K. *Bat Masterson: The Man and the Legend.* University of Oklahoma Press, Norman, OK, 1979, pg. 63.

24. Ibid., pg. 63. *Territory Times Bulletin,* October 7, 1958.

25. Ibid.

26. *Hutchinson News,* March 17, 1947.

27. DeArment, Robert K. *Bat Masterson: The Man and the Legend.* University of Oklahoma Press, Norman, OK, 1979, pg. 273-275. Miller, Nyle H., and Joseph W. Snell. *Great Gunfighters of the Kansas Cowtowns 1867-1886.* University of Nebraska Press, Lincoln, NE, 1963, pg. 193-212.

28. Ibid., pg. 56. DeArment, Robert K. *Bat Masterson: The Man and the Legend.* University of Oklahoma Press, Norman, OK, 1979, pg.

324-326. Herndon, Davis. *Palace Theatre & Gambling History.* Western Collection, Denver, CO, 1924.

29. Ancestry.com, Emma Walter. Penn, Chris. "Bat Masterson's Emma," *Wild West Magazine,* April 2012.

30. *Mills County Tribune,* August 29, 1895.

31. Breihan, Carl W. "They Call Him 'Bat,'" *Old Timers Wild West,* October 1978, No. 4.

32. *Lethbridge Herald,* July 15, 1932.

33. Breihan, Carl W. "They Call Him 'Bat,'" *Old Timers Wild West,* October 1978, No. 4.

Lotta Crabtree

1. *New York Times,* September 16, 1884.

2. Ibid. *Bridgeport Telegram,* July 2, 1925.

3. *Olean Weekly Democrat,* August 15, 1893.

4. *American Weekly,* April 3, 1949. *Oakland Tribune,* September 9, 1906.

5. Ibid.

6. Ibid.

7. *Daily Democrat,* December 12, 1879. *Burlington Hawkeye,* July 20, 1883. *Decatur Weekly Republican,* October 5, 1883.

8. *Bridgeport Telegram,* July 2, 1925.

9. *New York Times,* September 16, 1884.

10. Ibid.

11. Ibid.

12. Ibid.

13. Ibid.

14. Ibid.

15. Ibid.

16. *Independent Press Telegram, Southland Magazine,* October 22, 1949.

17. Place, Marian T. *Lotta Crabtree: Gold Rush Girl.* Bobb-Merrill Company, Inc., New York, NY, 1958, pg. 13-19.

18. *Oakland Tribune,* September 9, 1906. Chartier, JoAnn, and Chris Enss. *With Great Hope.* Globe Pequot Press, Guilford, CT, 2000, pg. 34-38. Dempsey, David, and Raymond R. Baldwin. *Triumph and Trials of Lotta Crabtree.* William Morrow Co., New York, NY, 1968, pg. 16-21.

19. Ibid., pg. 38-52.

20. Place, Marian T. *Lotta Crabtree: Gold Rush Girl.* Bobb-Merrill Company, Inc., New York, NY, 1958, pg. 48-63. Lardner, W. B., and M. J. Brock. *History of Placer & Nevada Counties.* Historic Record Co., Los Angeles, CA, 1924, pg. 321-324.

21. Place, Marian T. *Lotta Crabtree: Gold Rush Girl.* Bobb-Merrill Company, Inc., New York, NY, 1958, pg. 64-82.

22. Ibid., pg. 84-92. *American Weekly,* April 3, 1949. *Independent Press Telegram, Southland Magazine,* October 22, 1949.

23. *American Weekly,* April 3, 1949.

24. Dempsey, David, and Raymond R. Baldwin. *Triumph and Trials of Lotta Crabtree.* William Morrow Co., New York, NY, 1968, pg. 112-115.

25. Ibid., pg. 118-121.

26. Ibid.

27. *American Weekly,* April 3, 1949.

28. Ibid.

29. *Independent Press Telegram, Southland Magazine,* October 22, 1949.

30. Dempsey, David, and Raymond R. Baldwin. *Triumph and Trials of Lotta Crabtree.* William Morrow Co., New York, NY, 1968, pg. 120-125. Place, Marian T. *Lotta Crabtree: Gold Rush Girl.* Bobb-Merrill Company, Inc., New York, NY, 1958, pg. 139-147.

31. *Oakland Tribune,* September 9, 1906.

32. *Olean Weekly Democrat,* August 15, 1893.

33. Dempsey, David, and Raymond R. Baldwin. *Triumph and Trials of Lotta Crabtree.* William Morrow Co., New York, NY, 1968, pg. 126-132.

34. *Olean Weekly Democrat,* August 15, 1893.

35. Ibid. Dempsey, David, and Raymond R. Baldwin. *Triumph and Trials of Lotta Crabtree.* William Morrow Co., New York, NY, 1968, pg. 130-133.

Maria Josefa Jaramillo

1. Guild, Thelma S., and Harvey L. Carter. *Kit Carson: A Pattern for Heroes.* University of Nebraska Press, Lincoln, NE, 1984, pg. 71-74. *Taos News,* October 19, 2006. *Coronado Cuarto Centennial Edition, Albuquerque Journal,* April 30, 1940.

2. *Rio Rancho Observer,* May 16, 1907.

3. Guild, Thelma S., and Harvey L. Carter. *Kit Carson: A Pattern for Heroes.* University of Nebraska Press, Lincoln, NE, 1984, pg. 44. Dunlay, Tom. *Kit Carson & the Indians.* University of Nebraska Press, Lincoln, NE, 2000, pg. 93.

4. Ancestry.com, Maria Josefa Jaramillo. *Taos News,* October 19, 2006.

5. *Coronado Cuarto Centennial Edition, Albuquerque Journal,* April 30, 1940.

6. Ibid.

7. Carson, Kit, and Milo M. Quaife. *Kit Carson's Own Story of His Life.* The Narrative Press, Santa Barbara, CA, 1847, pg. 9-12.

8. *Rio Rancho Observer,* May 16, 1987.

9. Crutchfield, James A., Bill O'Neal, and Dale L. Walker. *Legends of the Wild West.* Publications International, Ltd., Lincolnwood, IL, 1995, pg. 38-43. Guild, Thelma S., and Harvey L. Carter. *Kit Carson: A Pattern for Heroes.* University of Nebraska Press, Lincoln, NE, 1984, pg. 65.

10. Carson, Kit, and Milo M. Quaife. *Kit Carson's Own Story of His Life.* The Narrative Press, Santa Barbara, CA, 1847, pg. 34-35.

11. Ibid.

12. Ibid.

13. *Taos News,* October 19, 2006.

14. *Boston Globe,* September 22, 1905.

15. Sabin, Edwin. *Kit Carson Days.* Nabu Press, Charleston, SC, 2009, pg. 78-86.

16. Preuss, Charles. *Exploring with Fremont.* University of Oklahoma. Norman, OK, 1958, pg. 112-115.

17. Ibid., pg. 84. Guild, Thelma S., and Harvey L. Carter. *Kit Carson: A Pattern for Heroes.* University of Nebraska Press, Lincoln, NE, 1984, pg. 97. Dunlay, Tom. *Kit Carson & the Indians.* University of Nebraska Press, Lincoln, NE, 2000, pg. 92-96.

18. Ibid., pg. 146-158.

19. Crutchfield, James A., Bill O'Neal, and Dale L. Walker. *Legends of the Wild West.* Publications International, Ltd., Lincolnwood, IL, 1995, pg. 38-41.

20. Ibid., pg. 38. Ancestry.com, Maria Josefa Jaramillo. Guild, Thelma S., and Harvey L. Carter. *Kit Carson: A Pattern for Heroes.* University of Nebraska Press, Lincoln, NE, 1984, pg. 134.

21. Ibid., pg. 185.

22. *Napa County Reporter,* March 13, 1875.

23. Crutchfield, James A., Bill O'Neal, and Dale L. Walker. *Legends of the Wild West.* Publications International, Ltd., Lincolnwood, IL, 1995, pg. 38-41.

24. Ibid., pg. 42-43.

25. Ibid., pg. 68-78.

26. *Taos News,* October 19, 2006. *Coronado Cuarto Centennial Edition, Albuquerque Journal,* April 30, 1940.

27. Chacon, Rafael. *Memories of Rafael Chacon.* Yucca Tree Press, Mexico City, Mexico, 1912, pg. 49. Sabin, Edwin. *Kit Carson Days.* Nabu Press, Charleston, SC, 2009, pg. 398.

28. Dunlay, Tom. *Kit Carson & the Indians.* University of Nebraska Press, Lincoln, NE, 2000, pg. 92-93.

29. Ibid., pg. 93.

30. Guild, Thelma S., and Harvey L. Carter. *Kit Carson: A Pattern for Heroes.* University of Nebraska Press, Lincoln, NE, 1984, pg. 222. Sabin, Edwin. *Kit Carson Days.* Nabu Press, Charleston, SC, 2009, pg. 179-184.

31. Ancestry.com, Maria Josefa Jaramillo. *Taos News,* October 19, 2006. *Coronado Cuarto Centennial Edition, Albuquerque Journal,* April 30, 1940.

32. *Advocate News,* May 26, 1968. Crutchfield, James A., Bill O'Neal, Dale L. Walker. *Legends of the Wild West.* Publications International, Ltd., Lincolnwood, IL, 1995, pg. 43.

33. Guild, Thelma S., and Harvey L. Carter. *Kit Carson: A Pattern for Heroes.* University of Nebraska Press, Lincoln, NE, 1984, pg. 279.

34. *Nuestras Raices Journal,* Vol. 5, No. 4, Winter Issue, 1962. Crutchfield, James A., Bill O'Neal, and Dale L. Walker. *Legends of the Wild West.* Publications International, Ltd., Lincolnwood, IL, 1995, pg. 38-45. *Taos News,* October 19, 2006. *Coronado Cuarto Centennial Edition, Albuquerque Journal,* April 30, 1940.

35. Ibid.

36. *Decatur Review,* June 4, 1868.

Luzena Stanley Wilson

1. Reiter, Joan S. *The Women.* Time-Life Series, Time-Life Books, Alexandria, VA, 1978, pg. 131-134. Fern, Hency. *My Checkered Life: Luzena Stanley Wilson in Early California.* Carl Mautz Publishing, Nevada City,

CA, 2003, pg. 8-15. Wilson, Luzena S. *Luzena Stanley Wilson, 49er.* Dodo Press, Bel Air, CA, 2010, pg. 12-21.

2. Reiter, Joan S. *The Women.* Time-Life Series, Time-Life Books, Alexandria, VA, 1978, pg. 131-134. Wilson, Luzena S. *Luzena Stanley Wilson, 49er.* Dodo Press, Bel Air, CA, 2010, pg. 12-21.

3. Levy, Jo Ann. *They Saw the Elephant.* Archon Books, Hamden, CT, 1990, pg. 4, 18.

4. Faragher, John M. *Women and Men on the Overland Trail.* Yale University Press, New Haven, CT, 1979, pg. 34-36, 77, 83. Wilson, Luzena S. *Luzena Stanley Wilson, 49er.* Dodo Press, Bel Air, CA, 2010, pg. 45-57.

5. Ibid.

6. Reiter, Joan S. *The Women.* Time-Life Series, Time-Life Books, Alexandria, VA, 1978, pg. 131-134.

7. Wilson, Luzena S. *Luzena Stanley Wilson, 49er.* Dodo Press, Bel Air, CA, 2010, pg. 45-57. Levy, Jo Ann. *They Saw the Elephant.* Archon Books, Hamden, CT, 1990, pg. 4, 18.

8. *Oakland Tribune,* May 23, 1937. Wilson, Luzena S. *Luzena Stanley Wilson, 49er.* Dodo Press, Bel Air, CA, 2010, pg. 89-92.

9. Wilson, Luzena S. *Luzena Stanley Wilson, 49er.* Dodo Press, Bel Air, CA, 2010, pg. 59-66. Levy, Jo Ann. *They Saw the Elephant.* Archon Books, Hamden, CT, 1990, pg. 4, 18, 98. Butruille, Susan G. *Women's Voices from the Western Frontier.* Tamarack Books, Boise, ID, 1995, pg. 117-119.

10. Wilson, Luzena S. *Luzena Stanley Wilson, 49er.* Dodo Press, Bel Air, CA, 2010, pg. 59-66.

11. Ibid. Reiter, Joan S. *The Women.* Time-Life Series, Time-Life Books, Alexandria, VA, 1978, pg. 131-134.

12. Ibid. *Oakland Tribune,* May 23, 1937.

13. Ibid.

14. Levy, Jo Ann. *They Saw the Elephant.* Archon Books, Hamden, CT, 1990, pg. 102-103.

15. Ibid. Wilson, Luzena S. *Luzena Stanley Wilson, 49er.* Dodo Press, Bel Air, CA, 2010, pg. 72-89.

16. Ibid.

17. Ibid. *Sacramento Transcript,* July 27, 1850.

18. Wilson, Luzena S. *Luzena Stanley Wilson, 49er.* Dodo Press, Bel Air, CA, 2010, pg. 72-89. Butruille, Susan G. *Women's Voices from the Western Frontier.* Tamarack Books, Boise, ID, 1995, pg. 117-119.

19. Reiter, Joan S. *The Women.* Time-Life Series, Time-Life Books, Alexandria, VA, 1978, pg. 131-134. Levy, Jo Ann. *They Saw the Elephant.* Archon Books, Hamden, CT, 1990, pg. 102-106.

20. Faragher, John M. *Women and Men on the Overland Trail.* Yale University Press, New Haven, CT, 1979, pg. 82-84. Wilson, Luzena S. *Luzena Stanley Wilson, 49er.* Dodo Press, Bel Air, CA, 2010, pg. 72-89.

21. Ibid.

22. Ibid.

23. Ibid. Reiter, Joan. *The Women.* Time-Life Series, Time-Life Books, Alexandria, VA, 1978, pg. 131-134. Levy, Jo Ann. *They Saw the Elephant.* Archon Books, Hamden, CT, 1990, pg. 122-128.

24. *Oakland Tribune,* May 23, 1937.

25. Reiter, Joan S. *The Women.* Time-Life Series, Time-Life Books, Alexandria, VA, 1978, pg. 131-134. Levy, Jo Ann. *They Saw the Elephant.* Archon Books, Hamden, CT, 1990, pg. 122-128.

26. Faragher, John M. *Women and Men on the Overland Trail.* Yale University Press, New Haven, CT, 1979, pg. 112-127.

27. *Oakland Tribune,* May 23, 1937.

28. Reiter, Joan S. *The Women.* Time-Life Series, Time-Life Books, Alexandria, VA, 1978, pg. 131-134.

29. *Woodland Daily Democrat,* July 12, 1902.

Zoe Agnes Stratton

1. Tilghman, Zoe. *Outlaw Days*. Harlow Publishing Company, Oklahoma City, OK, 1926, pg. 1-5. *Oakland Tribune,* December 6, 1959.

2. Ibid. Ancestry.com, William Tilghman.

3. Masterson, W. B. *Famous Gunfighters of the Western Frontier.* The Frontier Press, Houston, TX, 1957, pg. 42-53.

4. *Ada Evening News,* April 16, 1960.

5. Tilghman, Zoe. *Outlaw Days*. Harlow Publishing Company, Oklahoma City, OK, 1926, pg. 1-5. Nash, Jay R. *Encyclopedia of Western Lawmen & Outlaws.* Paragon House, New York, NY, 1992, pg. 303.

6. Miller, Floyd. *Bill Tilghman: Marshal of the Last Frontier.* Doubleday & Company, Inc., Garden City, NY, 1968, pg. 13-16.

7. Ibid.

8. Ibid.

9. Masterson, W. B. *Famous Gunfighters of the Western Frontier.* The Frontier Press, Houston, TX, 1957, pg. 42-53.

10. *Dodge City Times,* July 21, 1877.

11. *Dodge City Times,* February 9, 1878. Masterson, W. B. *Famous Gunfighters of the Western Frontier.* The Frontier Press, Houston, TX, 1957, pg. 42-53.

12. Ibid. *Ford County Globe,* April 23, 1878.

13. Masterson, W. B. *Famous Gunfighters of the Western Frontier.* The Frontier Press, Houston, TX, 1957, pg. 42-53. Nash, Jay R. *Encyclopedia of Western Lawmen & Outlaws.* Paragon House, New York, NY, 1992, pg. 303.

14. Masterson, W. B. *Famous Gunfighters of the Western Frontier.* The Frontier Press, Houston, TX, 1957, pg. 42-53.

15. Miller, Nyle H., and Joseph W. Snell. *Great Gunfighters of the Kansas Cowtowns 1867–1886.* University of Nebraska Press, Lincoln, NE, 1963, pg. 422-429.

16. Miller, Floyd. *Bill Tilghman: Marshal of the Last Frontier.* Doubleday & Company, Inc., Garden City, NY, 1968, pg. 181-195.

17. Ibid.

18. Tilghman, Zoe. *Outlaw Days.* Harlow Publishing Company, Oklahoma City, OK, 1926, pg. 1-5. *Oakland Tribune,* December 6, 1959.

19. *Salt Lake Tribune,* February 16, 1964. *Ogden Standard–Examiner,* September 25, 1930.

20. *Ada Evening News,* April 10, 1960. *Ada Evening News,* April 25, 1960.

21. Ibid.

22. *Manitowoc Herald News,* October 26, 1924.

23. Ibid.

24. Tilghman, Zoe. *Outlaw Days.* Harlow Publishing Company, Oklahoma City, OK, 1926, pg. 1-5.

25. Miller, Floyd. *Bill Tilghman: Marshal of the Last Frontier.* Doubleday & Company, Inc., Garden City, NY. 1968, pg. 237-238. *Muskogee County Democrat,* May 21, 1926.

26. *Ada Evening News,* April 10, 1960. *Ada Evening News,* April 25, 1960. *San Antonio Express,* November 3, 1924.

Calamity Jane

1. Rezatto, Helen. *Tales of the Black Hills.* Fenwyn Press, Rapid City, SD, 1989, pg. 78-89.

2. Adams, Ramon, B. A. Botkin, and Natt N. Dodge. *The Book of the American West.* Simon & Schuster, New York, NY, 1963, pg. 156-159.

3. *Janesville Daily Gazette,* July 13, 1901.

4. Aikman, Duncan. *Calamity Jane and the Other Lady Wildcats.* University of Nebraska, Lincoln, NE, 1927, pg. 82-87.

5. Ibid., pg. 12-15.

6. *Weekly Call,* September 24, 1898.

7. Ibid.

8. Brown, Dee. *The Gentle Tamers.* University of Nebraska, Lincoln, NE, 1958, pg. 92, 256-257. Griske, Michael. *The Diaries of John Hunton: Made to Last, Written to Last, Sagas of the Western Frontier.* Heritage Books, Westminster, MD, 2005, pg. 83, 88.

9. Jane, Calamity. *The Life and Adventures of Calamity Jane.* Benediction Classics Oxford, Oxfordshire, England, 2011, pg. 110-121. *Weekly Call,* September 24, 1898.

10. Ibid. McLaird, James. *Calamity Jane: The Woman and the Legend.* University of Oklahoma, Norman, OK, 2005, pg. 24-25.

11. Aikman, Duncan. *Calamity Jane and the Other Lady Wildcats.* University of Nebraska, Lincoln, NE, 1927, pg. 47-49.

12. Nash, Jay R. *Encyclopedia of Western Lawmen & Outlaws.* Paragon House, New York, NY, 1992, pg. 63. Crutchfield, James A., Bill O'Neal, and Dale L. Walker. *Legends of the Wild West.* Publications International, Ltd., Lincolnwood, IL, 1995, pg. 121-122.

13. *Oakland Tribune,* October 7, 1928.

14. *Greely Tribune,* August 2, 1973. Jane, Calamity. *The Life and Adventures of Calamity Jane.* Benediction Classics Oxford, Oxfordshire, England, 2011, pg. 132-140.

15. Ibid. *Weekly Call,* September 24, 1898.

16. Krohn, Katherine. *Women of the Wild West.* Lerner Publishing Group, Minneapolis, MN, 2000, pg. 80-83. Jane, Calamity. *The Life and Adventures of Calamity Jane.* Benediction Classics Oxford, Oxfordshire, England, 2011, pg. 132-140. Reiter, Joan Swallow. *The Women.* Time-Life Series, Time-Life Books, Alexandria, VA, 1978, pg. 18, 158-159.

17. *Steubenville Herald,* February 28, 1896.

18. Ibid. *Janesville Daily Gazette,* July 13, 1901. Aikman, Duncan. *Calamity Jane and the Other Lady Wildcats.* University of Nebraska, Lincoln, NE, 1927, pg. 47-49.

19. *Hutchinson News Herald,* May 14, 1950. Jane, Calamity. *The Life and Adventures of Calamity Jane.* Benediction Classics Oxford, Oxfordshire, England, 2011, pg. 153-159.

20. *Hutchinson News Herald,* May 14, 1950.

21. Vestal, Stanley. *Dodge City: Queen of Cowtowns.* Harper & Brothers, New York, NY, 1952, pg. 56-62. *Weekly Call,* September 24, 1898.

22. *Oakland Tribune,* October 7, 1928.

23. *Sunset Magazine,* July 1922.

24. Alexander, Kent. *Legends of the Old West.* Friedman/Fairfax Publishers, New York, NY, 1994, pg. 84, 100. *Hutchinson News Herald,* May 14, 1950.

25. Ibid.

26. *Oakland Tribune,* October 7, 1928. *Anaconda Standard,* April 19, 1904.

27. *Janesville Daily Gazette,* July 13, 1901. Aikman, Duncan. *Calamity Jane and the Other Lady Wildcats.* University of Nebraska, Lincoln, NE, 1927, pg. 52-69.

28. *Helena Independent,* July 27, 1876.

29. *Steubenville Herald,* February 26, 1896.

30. *Hutchinson News Herald,* May 14, 1950.

31. Jane, Calamity. *The Life and Adventures of Calamity Jane.* Benediction Classics Oxford, Oxfordshire, England, 2011, pg. 153-159. *Oakland Tribune,* October 7, 1928.

32. Ibid. *Anaconda Standard,* April 19, 1904.

33. Nash, Jay R. *Encyclopedia of Western Lawmen & Outlaws.* Paragon House, New York, NY, 1992, pg. 63.

34. *Black Hills Daily Times,* August 10, 1903. Wheeler, E. L. *Calamity Jane: Heroine of the Whoop-Up.* Beadle Pocket Library, Vol. V, No. 57, 1885.

35. *Hutchinson News Herald,* May 14, 1950. *Janesville Daily Gazette,* July 13, 1901.

Geronimo's Wives

1. Geronimo and S. M. Barrett. *Geronimo: His Own Story.* Ballantine Books, New York, NY, 1970, pg. 69-74. Aleshire, Peter. *The Fox and the Whirlwind: General George Crook & Geronimo.* John Wiley & Sons, Inc., New York, NY, 2000, pg. 28-34.

2. Geronimo and S. M. Barrett. *Geronimo: His Own Story.* Ballantine Books, New York, NY, 1970, pg. 74-83. Aleshire, Peter. *The Fox and the Whirlwind: General George Crook & Geronimo.* John Wiley & Sons, Inc., New York, NY, 2000, pg. 28-34. Faulk, Odie B. *The Geronimo Campaign.* Oxford University Press, New York, NY, 1969, pg. 20-21.

3. Geronimo and S. M. Barrett. *Geronimo: His Own Story.* Ballantine Books, New York, NY, 1970, pg. 74-83.

4. Ibid.

5. Aleshire, Peter. *The Fox and the Whirlwind: General George Crook & Geronimo.* John Wiley & Sons, Inc., New York, NY, 2000, pg. 28-34. Faulk, Odie B. *The Geronimo Campaign.* Oxford University Press, New York, NY, 1969, pg. 20-21.

6. Geronimo and S. M. Barrett. *Geronimo: His Own Story.* Ballantine Books, New York, NY, 1970, pg. 74-83.

7. Ibid. *Lawton Constitution & Morning Press,* January 27, 1957. *Postville Review,* March 5, 1909.

8. Ibid. Geronimo and S. M. Barrett. *Geronimo: His Own Story.* Ballantine Books, New York, NY, 1970, pg. 91-93.

9. Aleshire, Peter. *The Fox and the Whirlwind: General George Crook & Geronimo.* John Wiley & Sons, Inc., New York, NY, 2000, pg. 61-87.

10. Geronimo and S. M. Barrett. *Geronimo: His Own Story.* Ballantine Books, New York, NY, 1970, pg. 101-103.

11. Ibid., pg. 112.

12. Ibid., pg. 112-116. Aleshire, Peter. *The Fox and the Whirlwind: General George Crook & Geronimo*. John Wiley & Sons, Inc., New York, NY, 2000, pg. 61-87.

13. Geronimo and S. M. Barrett. *Geronimo: His Own Story*. Ballantine Books, New York, NY, 1970, pg. 138-140.

14. Ibid., pg. 228-230. Capps, Benjamin. *The Indians*. Time-Life Books, New York, NY, 1973, pg. 54.

15. Aleshire, Peter. *The Fox and the Whirlwind: General George Crook & Geronimo*. John Wiley & Sons, Inc., New York, NY, 2000, pg. 228-230. Capps, Benjamin. *The Great Chiefs*. Time-Life Books, New York, NY, 1975, pg. 60-87.

16. Geronimo and S. M. Barrett. *Geronimo: His Own Story*. Ballantine Books, New York, NY, 1970, pg. 138-140. Aleshire, Peter. *The Fox and the Whirlwind: General George Crook & Geronimo*. John Wiley & Sons, Inc., New York, NY, 2000, pg. 228-230. Capps, Benjamin. *The Great Chiefs*. Time-Life Books, New York, NY, 1975, pg. 60-87.

17. Geronimo and S. M. Barrett. *Geronimo: His Own Story*. Ballantine Books, New York, NY, 1970, pg. 120-125. *Pharos Tribune*. November 22, 1992. *Biloxi Daily Herald*, June 27, 1900.

18. *Gallup Independent*, July 7, 1950. *Casa Grande Valley Dispatch*, March 15, 1928. Aleshire, Peter. *The Fox and the Whirlwind: General George Crook & Geronimo*. John Wiley & Sons, Inc., New York, NY, 2000, pg. 274-282.

19. Ibid.

20. *Spirit Lake Beacon*, July 2, 1886.

21. *Eau Claire News*, May 24, 1884. Geronimo and S. M. Barrett. *Geronimo: His Own Story*. Ballantine Books, New York, NY, 1970, pg. 136-139.

22. *Galveston News*, September 27, 1886.

23. *Gallup Independent*, July 7, 1950.

24. Ibid.

Eleanora Dumont

1. *Oakland Tribune,* September 26, 1937. Zauner, Phyllis. *Those Spirited Women of the Early West.* Zanel Publications, Sonoma, CA, 1989, 49-50. Aikman, Duncan. *Madam Mustache and Other Gaming Ladies.* Henry Holt & Co., New York, NY, 1948, pg. 108-110. Kelly, Bill. *Gamblers of the Old West.* B&F Enterprises, Las Vegas, NV, 1995, pg. 65-70. Nash, Jay R. *Encyclopedia of Western Lawmen & Outlaws.* Paragon House, New York, NY, 1992, pg. 108-109.

2. Ibid.

3. *Logansport Journal,* July 6, 1859.

4. Nash, Jay R. *Encyclopedia of Western Lawmen & Outlaws.* Paragon House, New York, NY, 1992, pg. 108-109. Enss, Chris. *Pistol Packin' Madams: True Stories of Notorious Women of the Old West.* TwoDot, Guilford, CT, 2006, pg. 9-16.

5. Ibid. Seagraves, Anne. *Women of the Sierra.* Wesanne Enterprises, Lakeport, CA, 1990, pg. 163-166.

6. *American Weekly,* September 19, 1940. *Oakland Tribune,* December 9, 1928.

7. Ibid.

8. *Oakland Tribune,* December 9, 1928. Aikman, Duncan. *Madam Mustache and Other Gaming Ladies.* Henry Holt & Co., New York, NY, 1948, pg. 108-110.

9. *Oakland Tribune,* December 9, 1928.

10. Nash, Jay R. *Encyclopedia of Western Lawmen & Outlaws.* Paragon House, New York, NY, 1992, pg. 108-109. Enss, Chris. *Pistol Packin' Madams: True Stories of Notorious Women of the Old West.* TwoDot, Guilford, CT, 2006, pg. 9-16. Seagraves, Anne. *Women of the Sierra.* Wesanne Enterprises, Lakeport, CA, 1990, pg. 163-166.

11. *Territorial Enterprise,* December 19, 1858.

12. *Oakland Tribune,* September 26, 1937. Zauner, Phyllis. *Those Spirited Women of the Early West.* Zanel Publications, Sonoma, CA, 1989, 49-50.

13. Ibid.

14. Nash, Jay R. *Encyclopedia of Western Lawmen & Outlaws.* Paragon House, New York, NY, 1992; pg. 108-109.

15. *American Weekly,* September 19, 1940. *Oakland Tribune,* December 9, 1928.

16. Ibid.

17. Drago, Harry S. *Notorious Ladies of the Frontier.* Ballantine Books, New York, NY, 1972, pg. 12-15.

18. Nash, Jay R. *Encyclopedia of Western Lawmen & Outlaws.* Paragon House, New York, NY, 1992, pg. 108-109. Enss, Chris. *Pistol Packin' Madams: True Stories of Notorious Women of the Old West.* TwoDot, Guilford, CT, 2006, pg. 9-16. Seagraves, Anne. *Women of the Sierra.* Wesanne Enterprises, Lakeport, CA, 1990, pg. 163-166.

19. *American Weekly,* September 19, 1940. *Oakland Tribune,* December 9, 1928.

20. Ibid.

21. Ibid.

22. *Sacramento Union,* September 18, 1879. Seagraves, Anne. *Women of the Sierra.* Wesanne Enterprises, Lakeport, CA, 1990, pg. 163-166.

23. *Oakland Tribune,* September 26, 1937. Zauner, Phyllis. *Those Spirited Women of the Early West.* Zanel Publications, Sonoma, CA, 1989, pg. 49-50. Aikman, Duncan. *Madam Mustache and Other Gaming Ladies.* Henry Holt & Co., New York, NY, 1948, pg. 108-110. Kelly, Bill. *Gamblers of the Old West.* B&F Enterprises, Las Vegas, NV, 1995, pg. 65-70. Nash, Jay R. *Encyclopedia of Western Lawmen & Outlaws.* Paragon House, New York, NY, 1992, pg. 108-109.

BIBLIOGRAPHY

Adams, Ramon, B. A. Botkin, and Natt N. Dodge. *The Book of the American West*. NY: Simon & Schuster, 1963.

Aikman, Duncan. *Calamity Jane and the Other Lady Wildcats*. Lincoln, NE: University of Nebraska, 1927.

———. *Madam Mustache and Other Gaming Ladies*. NY: Henry Holt & Company, 1948

Aleshire, Peter. *The Fox and the Whirlwind: General George Crook & Geronimo*. NY: John Wiley & Sons, Inc., 2000.

Alexander, Kent. *Legends of the Old West*. New York: Friedman/Fairfax Publishers, 1994.

Breihan, Carl W. "They Call Him 'Bat.'" *Old Timers Wild West*, no. 4, October 1978.

Brown, Dee. *The Gentle Tamers*. Lincoln, NE: University of Nebraska, 1958.

Burton, Doris K. *Queen Ann Bassett Alias Etta Place*. Fayetteville, TN: Burton Enterprises, 1992.

Butruille, Susan G. *Women's Voices from the Western Frontier*. Boise, ID: Tamarack Books, 1995.

Capps, Benjamin. *The Indians*. NY: Time-Life Books, 1973.

———. *The Great Chiefs*. NY: Time-Life Books, 1975.

Carson, Kit, and Milo M. Quaife. *Kit Carson's Own Story of His Life*. Santa Barbara, CA: The Narrative Press, 1847.

Chacon, Rafael. *Memories of Rafael Chacon*. Mexico City, Mexico: Yucca Tree Press, 1912.

Chartier, JoAnn, and Chris Enss. *With Great Hope*. Guilford, CT: Globe Pequot Press, 2000.

Crutchfield, James A., Bill O'Neal, and Dale L. Walker. *Legends of the Wild West*. Lincolnwood, IL: Publications International, 1995.

DeArment, Robert K. *Bat Masterson: The Man and the Legend*. Norman, OK: University of Oklahoma Press, 1979.

Dempsey, David, and Raymond R. Baldwin. *Triumph and Trials of Lotta Crabtree*. New York: William Morrow Company, 1968.

Drago, Harry S. *Notorious Ladies of the Frontier*. NY: Ballantine Books, 1972.

Dunlay, Tom. *Kit Carson & the Indians*. Lincoln, NE: University of Nebraska Press, 2000.

Enss, Chris. *Pistol Packin' Madams: True Stories of Notorious Women of the Old West*. Guilford, CT: TwoDot, 2006.

Faragher, John M. *Women and Men on the Overland Trail*. New Haven, CT: Yale University Press, 1979.

Faulk, Odie B. *The Geronimo Campaign*. NY: Oxford University Press, 1969.

Fern, Hency. *My Checkered Life: Luzena Stanley Wilson in Early California*. Nevada City, CA: Carl Mautz Publishing, 2003.

Fielder, Mildred. *Wild Bill & Deadwood*. Seattle, WA: Superior Publishing Company, 1965.

Fisher, Linda. *Agnes Lake Hickok: Queen of the Circus, Wife of a Legend*. Norman, OK: University of Oklahoma, 2009.

Fitzsimmons, Robert. *Encyclopedia Britannica*. United Kingdom, 2000.

Geronimo, and S. M. Barrett. *Geronimo: His Own Story*. NY: Ballantine Books, 1970.

Griske, Michael. *The Diaries of John Hunton: Made to Last, Written to Last, Sagas of the Western Frontier*. Westminster, MD: Heritage Books, 2005.

Guild, Thelma S., and Harvey L. Carter. *Kit Carson: A Pattern for Heroes*. Lincoln, NE: University of Nebraska Press, 1984.

Herndon, Davis. *Palace Theatre & Gambling History*. Denver, CO: Western Collection, 1924.

Houseworth, Thomas. *Tony Denier, the Celebrated Pantomimist*. New Haven, CT: Yale Books, 1910.

Jane, Calamity. *The Life and Adventures of Calamity Jane*. Oxfordshire, England: Benediction Classics Oxford, 2011.

Kelly, Bill. *Gamblers of the Old West*. Las Vegas, NV: B & F Enterprises, 1995.

Kirby, Edward. *The Saga of Butch Cassidy and the Wild Bunch.* Denver, CO: Filter Press, 1977.

Krohn, Katherine. *Women of the Wild West.* Minneapolis, MN: Lerner Publishing Group, 2000.

Lardner, W. B., and M. J. Brock. *History of Placer & Nevada Counties.* Los Angeles, Historic Record Co., 1924.

Levy, Jo Ann. *They Saw the Elephant.* Hamden, CT: Archon Books, 1990.

Masterson, W. B. *Famous Gunfighters of the Western Frontier.* Houston, TX: The Frontier Press, 1957.

McLaird, James. *Calamity Jane: The Woman and the Legend.* Norman, OK: University of Oklahoma, 2005.

McWhirter, Norris. *Guinness Book of World Records.* NY: Bantam Publishing, 1997.

Miller, Floyd. *Bill Tilghman: Marshal of the Last Frontier.* Garden City, NY: Doubleday & Company, Inc., 1968.

Miller, Frank E. *Indian Club Swinging.* Item available at the University of California Libraries. San Diego: CA, 1900.

Miller, Nyle H., and Joseph W. Snell. *Great Gunfighters of the Kansas Cowtowns 1867-1886.* Lincoln, NE: University of Nebraska Press, 1963.

Nash, Jay R. *Encyclopedia of Western Lawmen & Outlaws.* New York: Paragon House, 1992.

Penn, Chris. "Bat Masterson's Emma." *Wild West Magazine,* April 2012.

Place, Marian T. *Lotta Crabtree: Gold Rush Girl.* NY: Bobb-Merrill Company, Inc., 1958.

Preuss, Charles. *Exploring with Fremont.* Norman, OK: University of Oklahoma, 1958.

Reiter, Joan S., and the editors of Time-Life Books. *The Women.* Alexandria, VA: Time-Life Books, 1978.

Rezatto, Helen. *Tales of the Black Hills.* Rapid City, SD: Fenwyn Press, 1989.

Roberts, Phil. *Agnes Thatcher Lake: Equestrian Rider, Circus Performer, and Wild Bill's Wife.* Item available at the Department of History, University of Wyoming, 2007.

Rosa, Joseph. *They Called Him Bill*. Norman, OK: University of Oklahoma, 1964.

Rutter, Michael. *Wild Bunch Women*. Guilford, CT: TwoDot, 2003.

Sabin, Edwin. *Kit Carson Days*. Charleston, SC: Nabu Press, 2009.

Seagraves, Anne. *Women of the Sierra*. Lakeport, CA: Wesanne Enterprises, 1990.

Tilghman, Zoe. *Outlaw Days*. Oklahoma City, OK: Harlow Publishing Company, 1926.

Vestal, Stanley. *Dodge City: Queen of Cowtowns*. NY: Harper & Brothers, 1952.

Wilson, Gary. *A Tiger of the Wild Bunch*. Guilford, CT: TwoDot, 2007.

Wilson, Luzena S. *Luzena Stanley Wilson, 49er*. Bel Air, CA: Dodo Press, 2010.

Zauner, Phyllis. *Those Spirited Women of the Early West*. Sonoma, CA: Zanel Publications, 1989.

Newspapers & Journals

Ada Evening News. April 10, 1960. April 16, 1960. April 25, 1960.

Advocate News. May 26, 1968.

American Weekly. September 19, 1940. April 3, 1949. February 10, 1950.

Anaconda Standard. April 19, 1904.

Atlanta Journal Constitution. July 3 & 8, 1904.

Berkshire Eagle. November 4, 1958.

Biloxi Daily Herald. June 27, 1900.

Black Hills Daily Times. August 10, 1903.

Black Hills Pioneer. August 2, 1876.

Boston Globe. September 22, 1905.

Bridgeport Telegram. July 2, 1925.

Burlington Hawkeye. July 20, 1883.

Casa Grande Valley Dispatch. March 15, 1928.

Cedar Rapids Evening Gazette. September 3, 1907.

Cheyenne Daily Leader. March 7, 1876.

Chicago Daily Tribune. August 17, 1879.

Cleveland Sun News, The News Magazine Supplement. February 19, 1929.

Coronado Cuarto Centennial Edition, Albuquerque Journal. April 30, 1940.

Courier News. July 31, 1975.

Daily Democrat. December 12, 1879.

Daily Democrat Times. April 7, 1970.

Daily Free Press. October 13, 1879.

Decatur Review. June 4, 1868.

Decatur Weekly Republican. October 5, 1883.

Des Moines News. August 12, 1918.

Dodge City Times. July 21, 1877. February 9, 1878.

Eau Claire News. May 24, 1884.

Ford County Globe. April 23, 1878.

Gallup Independent. July 7, 1950.

Galveston News. September 27, 1886. January 22, 1907.

Greely Tribune. August 2, 1973.

Hawk-Eye. August 29, 1965.

Hays Daily News. August 1, 2001.

Helena Independent. July 27, 1876.

Hutchinson News. March 17, 1947.

Hutchinson News Herald. May 14, 1950.

Idaho State Journal. August 27, 1976.

Janesville Daily Gazette. July 13, 1901.

Lawton Constitution & Morning Press. January 27, 1957.

Lethbridge Herald. July 15, 1932.

Logansport Journal. July 6, 1859.

Los Angeles Times. April 7, 1970.

Manitowoc Herald News. October 26, 1924.

Mills County Tribune. August 29, 1895.

Muskogee County Democrat. May 21, 1926.

Napa County Reporter. March 13, 1875.

New York Clipper. October 28, 1879. October 7, 1882. January 17, 1891.

New York Times. September 16, 1884. April 17, 1893. August 22 & 23, 1907. March 19, 1935.

Nuestras Raices Journal. Winter Issue, Vol. 5, No. 4, 1962.

Oakland Tribune. September 9, 1906. October 7, 1928. December 9, 1928. May 23, 1937. September 26, 1937. December 6, 1959.

Ogden Standard-Examiner. September 25, 1930.

Olean Weekly Democrat. August 15, 1893.

Pharos Tribune. November 22, 1992.

Postville Review. March 5, 1909.

Register News. August 22, 1958.

Rio Rancho Observer. May 16, 1907.

Rocky Mountain News. April 21, 1884. March 15, 1889.

Sacramento Transcript. July 27, 1850.

Sacramento Union. September 18, 1879.

Salt Lake City Tribune. February 16, 1964.

San Antonio Express. November 3, 1924.

San Antonio Light. December 19, 1917.

Sandusky Daily Register. January 15, 1891.

Seattle Post Intelligencer. September 18, 1920.

Sioux City Sunday Journal. July 12, 1925.

Soda Springs News. September 8, 1877.

Spirit Lake Beacon. July 2, 1886.

Steubenville Herald. February 26, 1896.

Taos News. October 19, 2006.

Territorial Enterprise. December 19, 1858.

Territory Times Bulletin. October 7, 1958.

Tribune. August 29, 1929.

Washington Post. July 7, 1907.

Weekly Call. September 24, 1898.

Woodland Daily Democrat. July 12, 1902.

Websites

Clifton Family. Ancestry.com

Jaramillo, Maria Josefa. Ancestry.com

Moulton, Edwin. Ancestry.com

Tilghman, William. Ancestry.com

Walter, Emma. Ancestry.com

Periodicals & Other Print

Independent Press Telegram, Southland Magazine. October 22, 1949.

Montgomery Ward Company Pamphlet. Chicago, IL: 1886.

Sunset Magazine. July 1922.

Wheeler, E. L. *Calamity Jane: Heroine of the Whoop-Up.* Beadle Pocket Library Vol. V, No. 57, 1885 (Dime Novel).

ABOUT THE AUTHOR

Chris Enss is an author, scriptwriter, and comedienne who has written for television and film and performed on cruise ships and on stage. She has worked with award-winning musicians, writers, directors, producers, and as a screenwriter for Tricor Entertainment, but her passion is for telling the stories of the men and women who shaped the history and mythology of the American West. Some of the most famous names in history, not to mention film and popular culture, populate her books. She reveals the stories behind the many romances of William "Buffalo Bill" Cody who moved on from his career as a scout on the plains to bring the enormously successful performance spectacle of Buffalo Bill's Wild West to audiences throughout the United States and Europe between 1883 and 1916. And she tells the stories of the many talented and daring women who performed alongside men in the Wild West shows, who changed the way the world thought about women forever through the demonstration of their skills.

Chris brings her sensitive eye and respect for their work to her stories of more contemporary American entertainers, as well. Her books reveal the lives of John Wayne, Roy Rogers, and Dale Evans, bringing to light stories gleaned from family interviews and archives. The most famous American couple of the nineteenth century, General George Armstrong Custer and Elizabeth Bacon Custer, draws her scrutiny as well. *None Wounded, None Missing, All Dead* reveals the personality of the fiery, lively Libbie and her lifelong effort to burnish her husband's reputation. Chris takes readers along the trail with the Intrepid Posse as their horses thunder after the murderer of Dodge City dance hall favorite Dora Hand, and she turns her attention to the famous Sam Sixkiller, legendary Cherokee sheriff, but perhaps most extraordinary are the stories of the ordinary men and women who shaped American history when they came west as schoolmarms, gold miners, madams, and mail-order brides.